EASY to DRAW 3

I0489490

cartoon
ANIMALS

This Book Belongs to:

_____

SUNLIFE DRAWING

This book will **HELP** you **EASY TO DRAW** 26 different **CARTTOON ANIMALS**. Even if this is your first attempt at sketching, you will not face any difficultly in **DRAWING**, using easy to follow **STEP-BY-STEP** illustrations.

Also you will find **ALL** the **ANIMALS** for **FUN COLORING**. They are printed on one side of a page for easy removal and displaying of your own artistic work.

Enjoy **DRAWING & COLORING!**

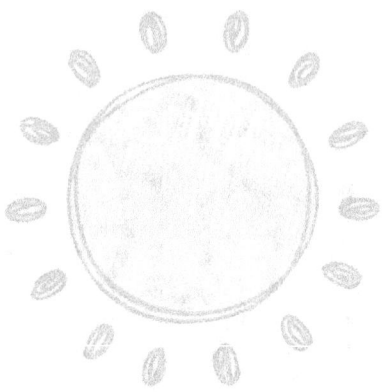

E-mail: SunlifeDrawing@gmail.com
Twitter: @SunlifeDrawing
Amazon Author's Page: Amazon.com/author/sunlifedrawing

CONTENTS:

Ant..................................4

Bear................................5

Cat.................................6

Dog.................................7

Elephant........................8

Frog................................9

Giraffe..........................10

Horse.............................11

Iguana...........................12

Jellyfish.........................13

Kangaroo.....................14

Lion...............................15

Monkey.........................16

Nightingale...............17

Owl...............................18

Pig................................19

Quail.............................20

Rabbit...........................21

Squirrel.........................22

Turtle.............................23

Urchin............................24

Viper..............................25

Wolf...............................26

X-Ray Fish..................27

Yak...............................28

Zebra.............................29

+ COLORING BOOK........31

Ant

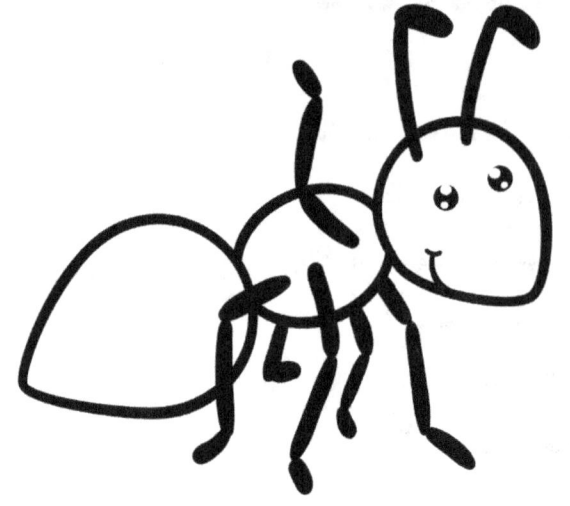

1.

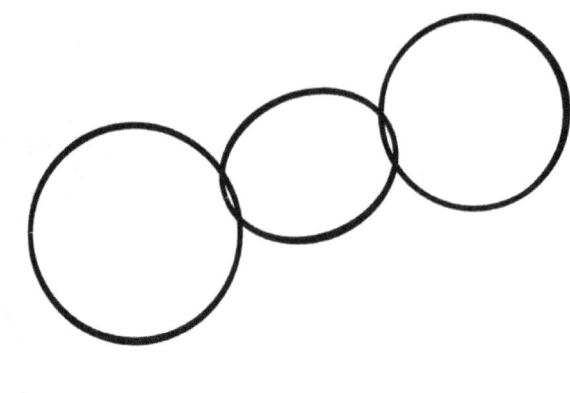

2.

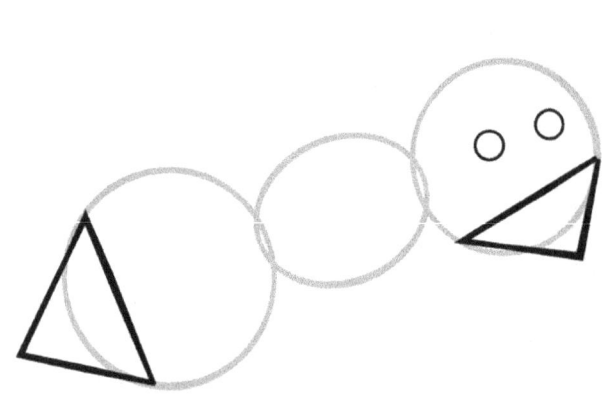

3.

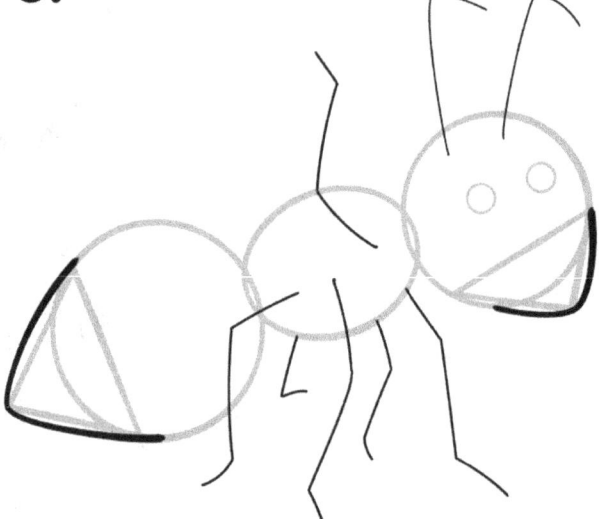

4.

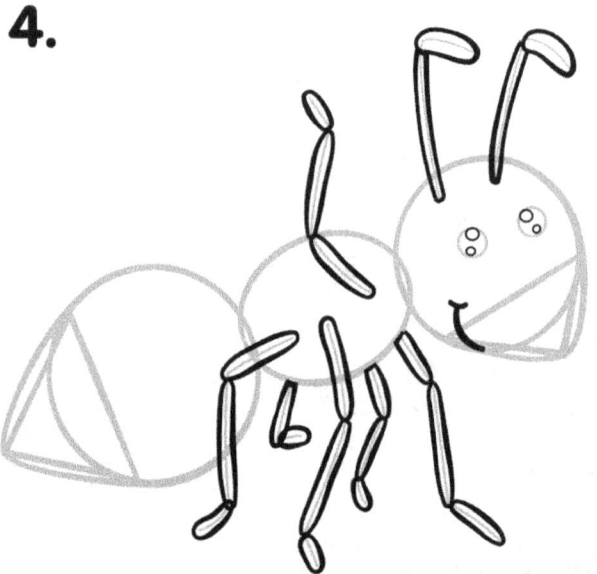

5.

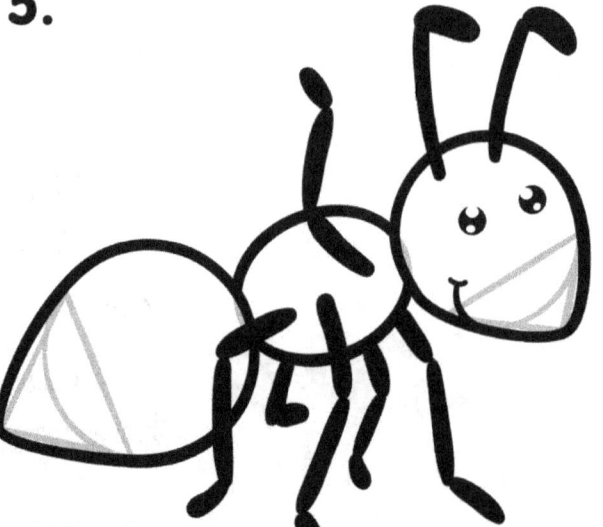

Bear

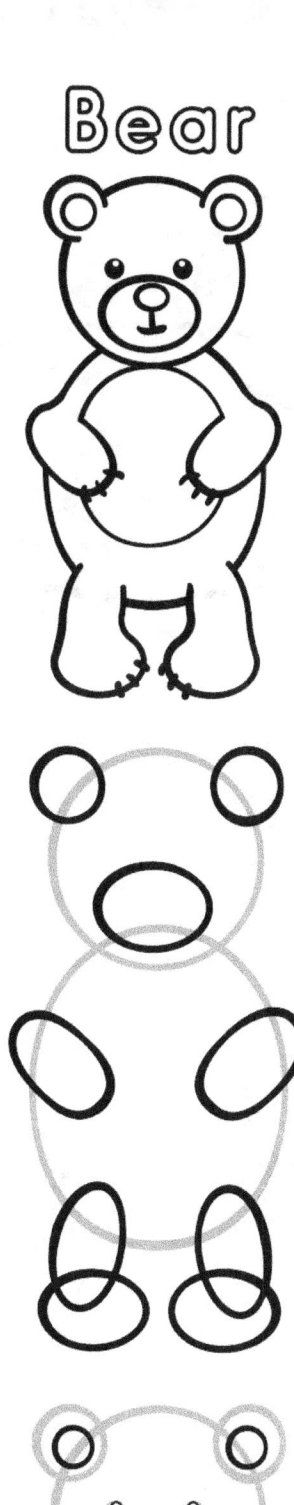

1.

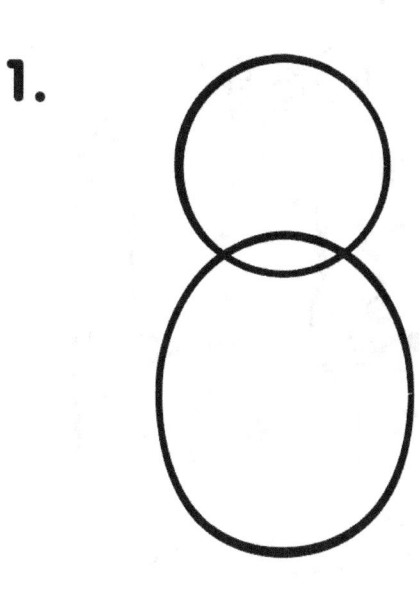

2.

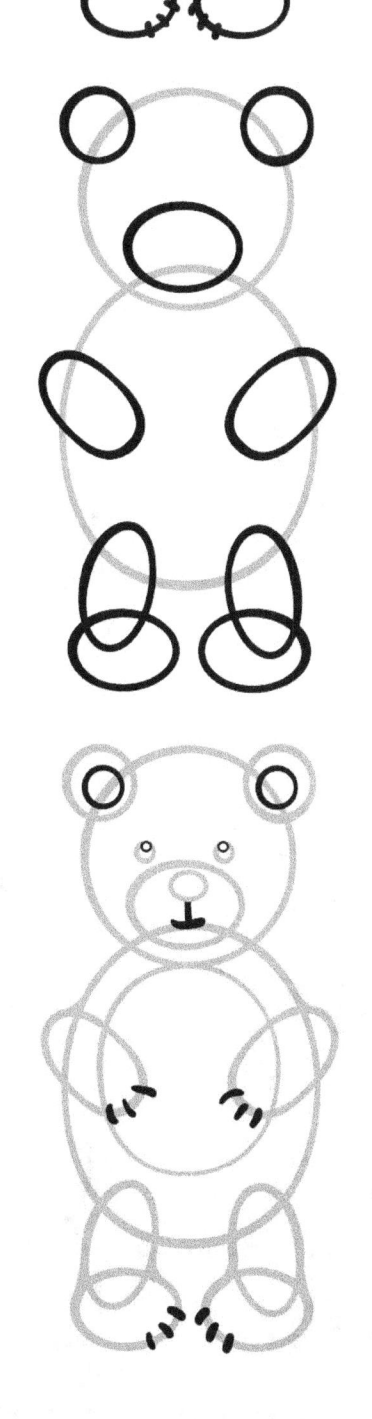

3.

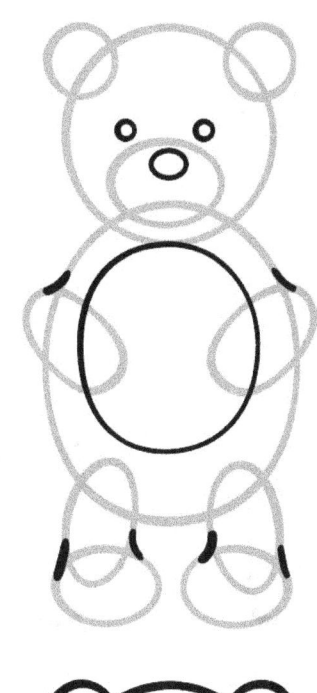

4.

5.

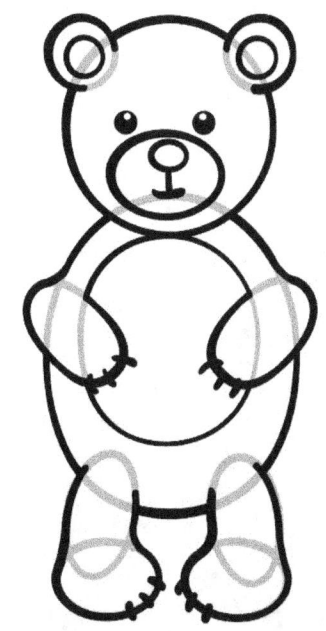

Cat

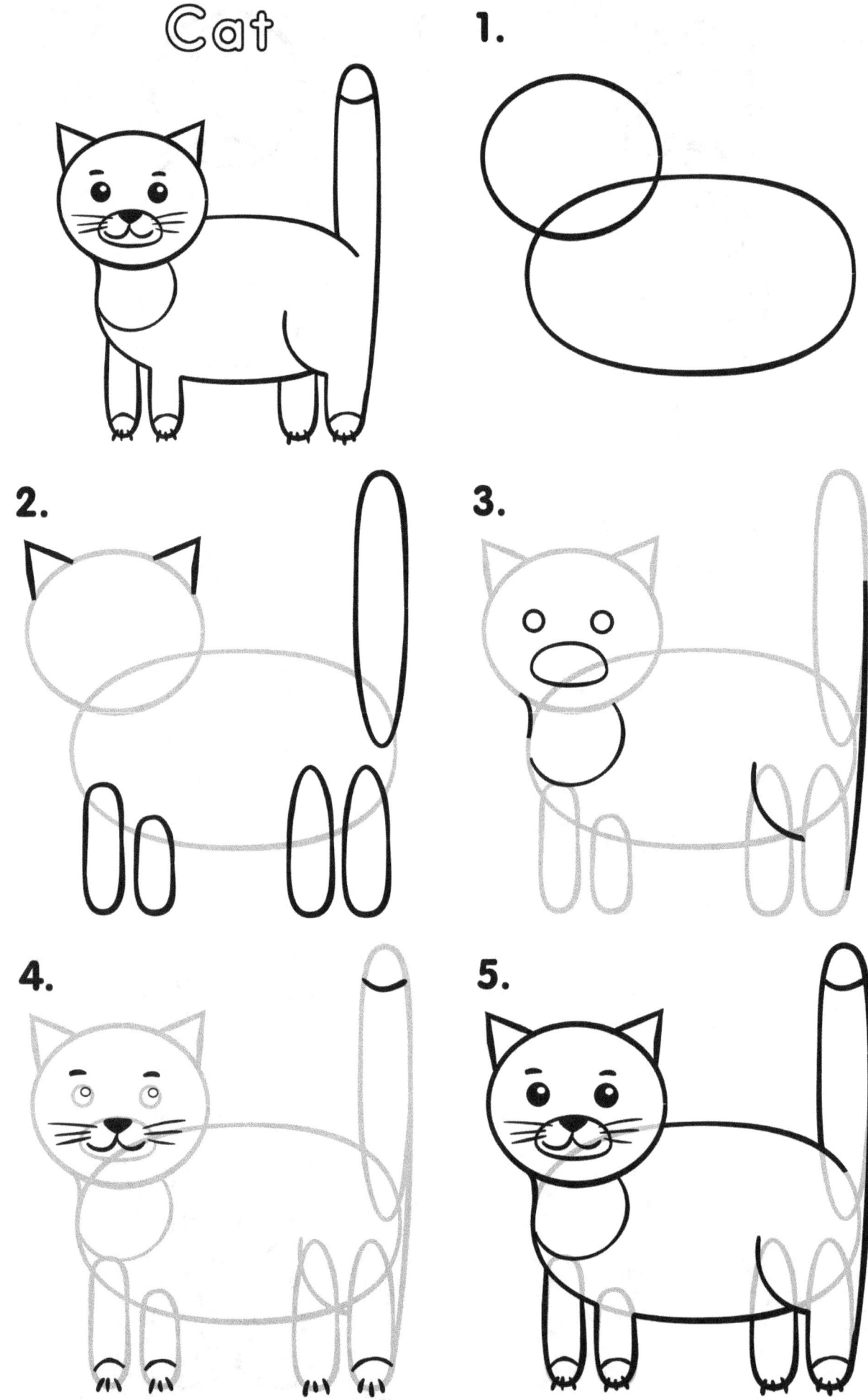

1.

2.

3.

4.

5.

Dog

1.

2.

3.

4.

5.

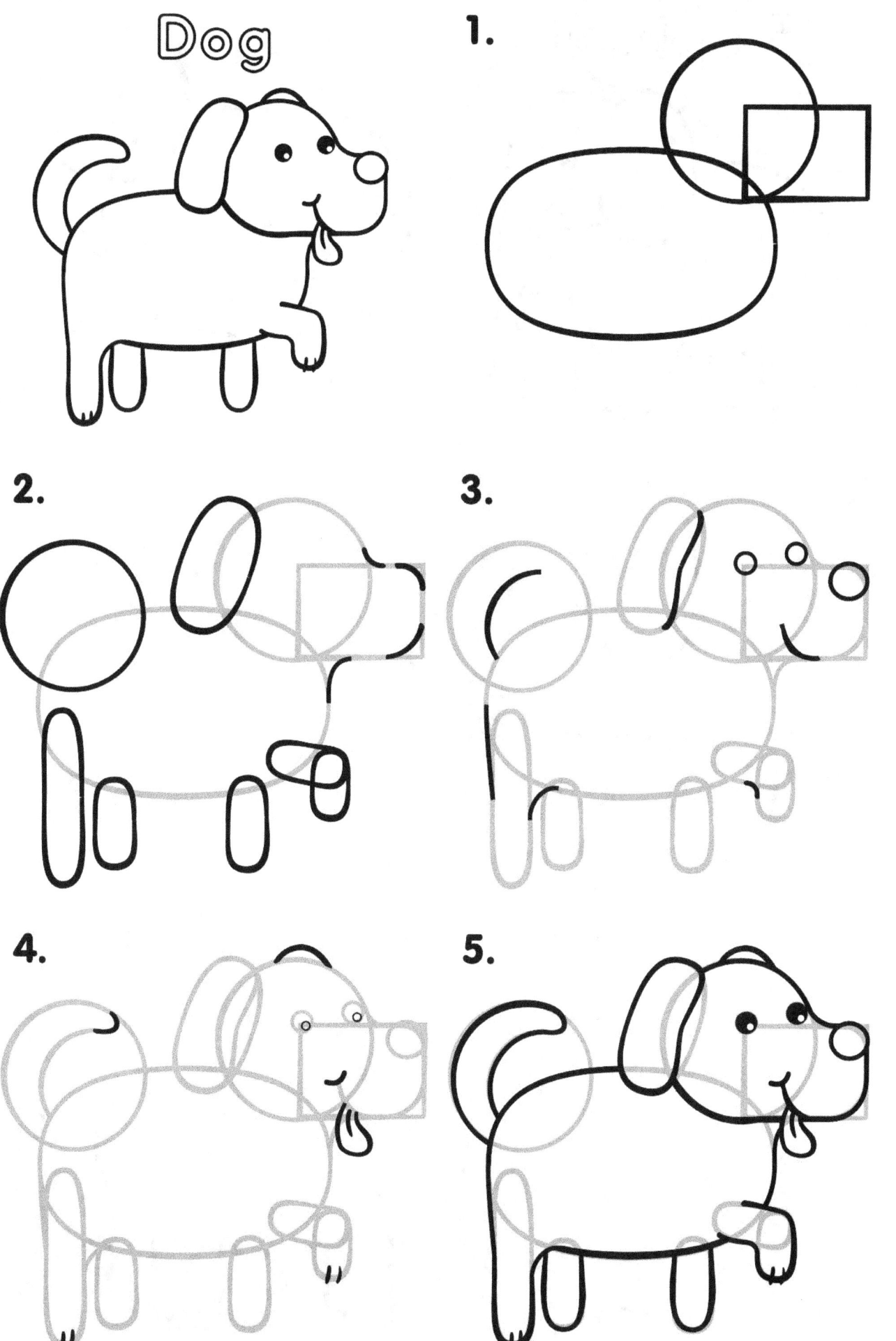

Elephant

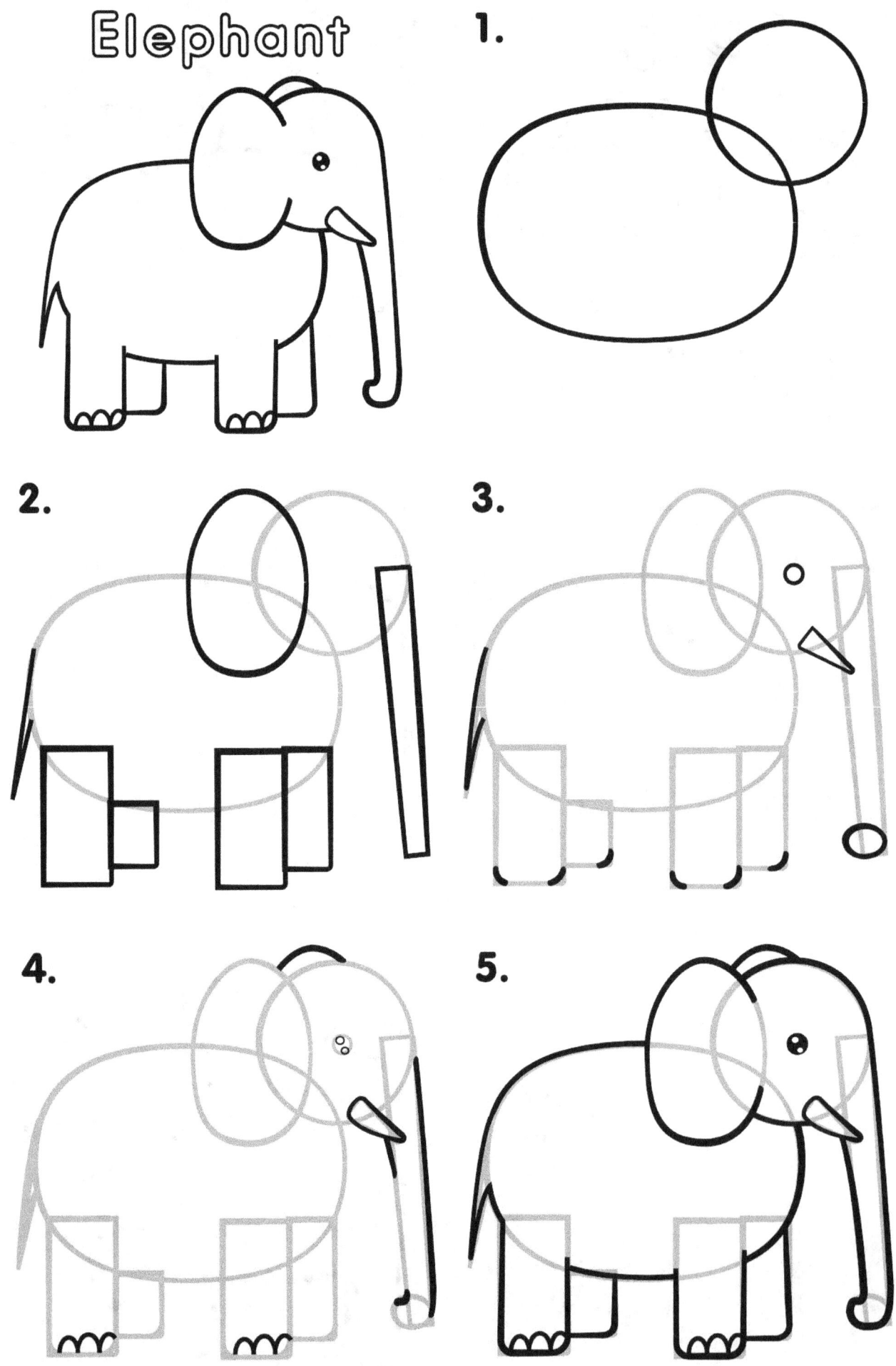

1.

2.

3.

4.

5.

Frog

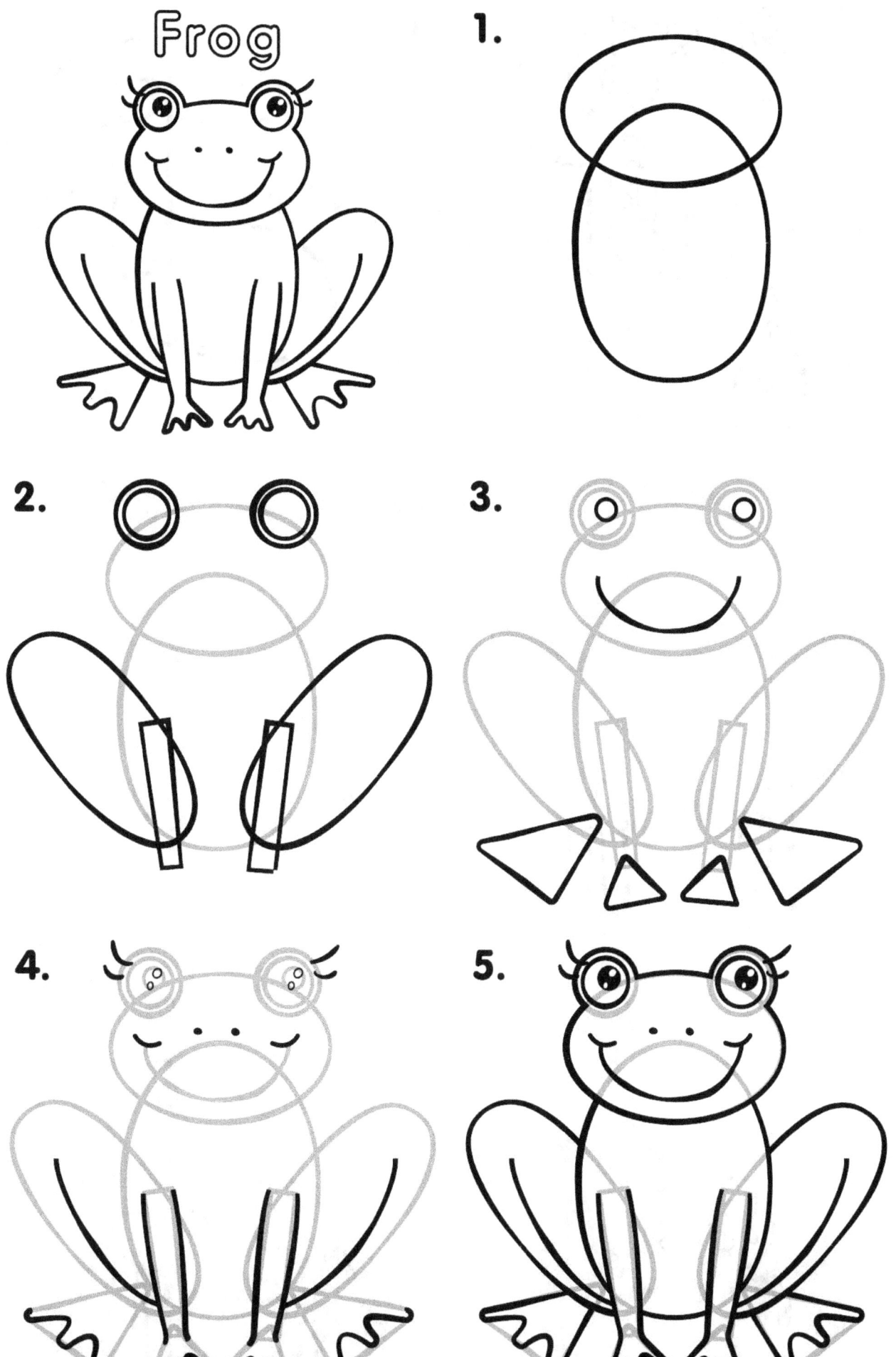

1.

2.

3.

4.

5.

Giraffe

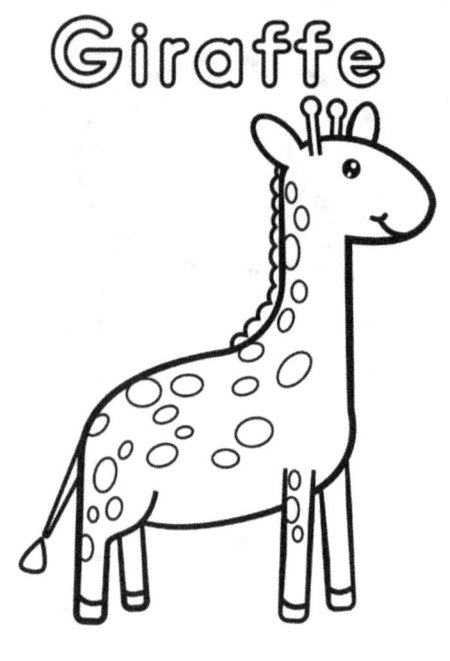

1.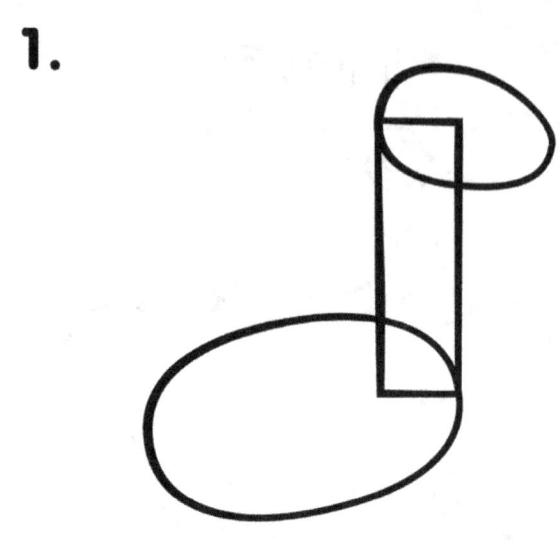

2.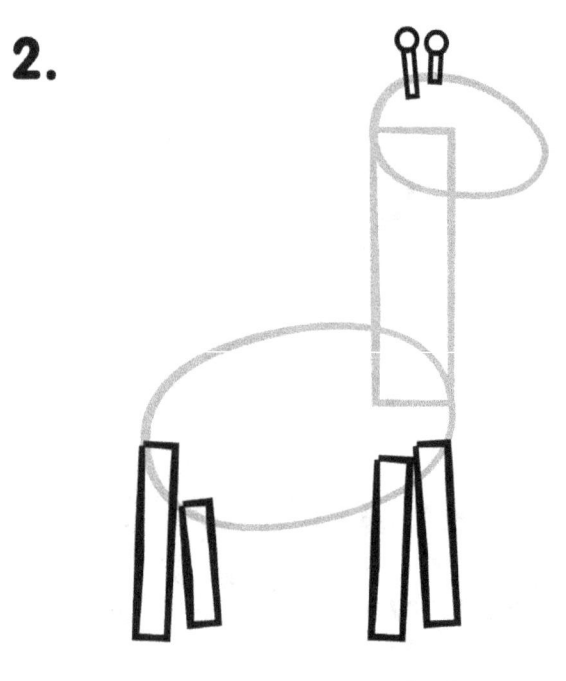

3.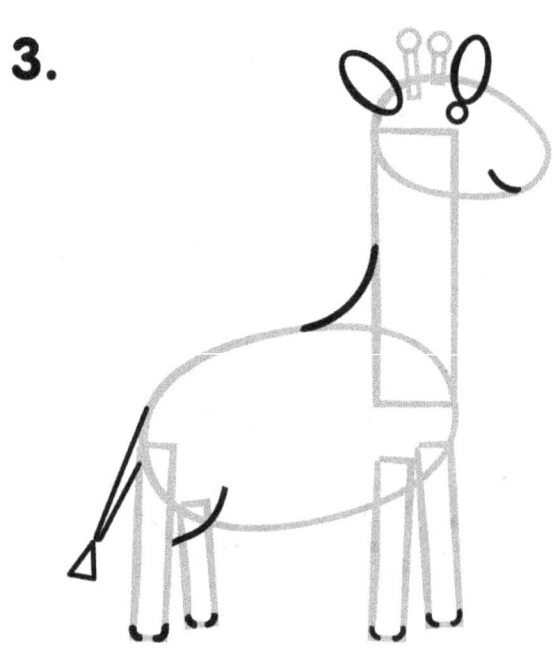

4.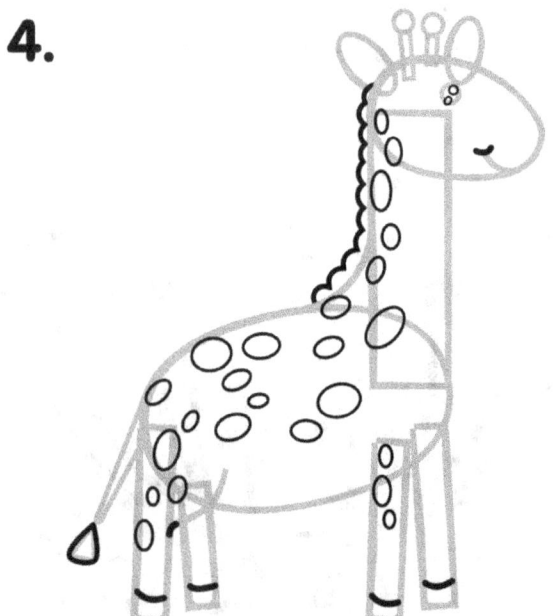

5.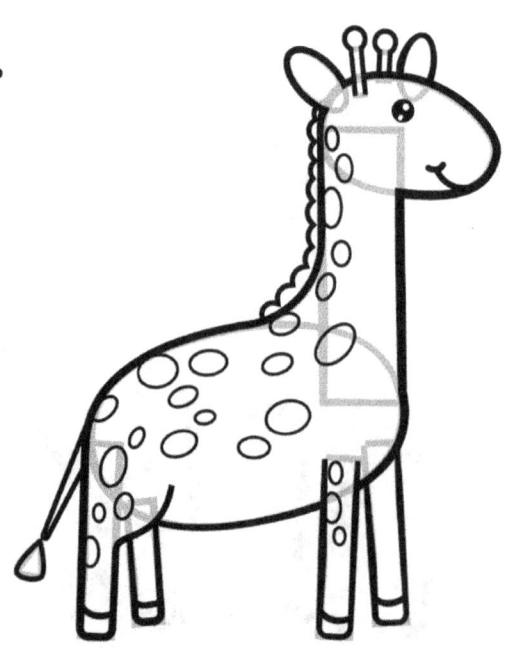

Horse

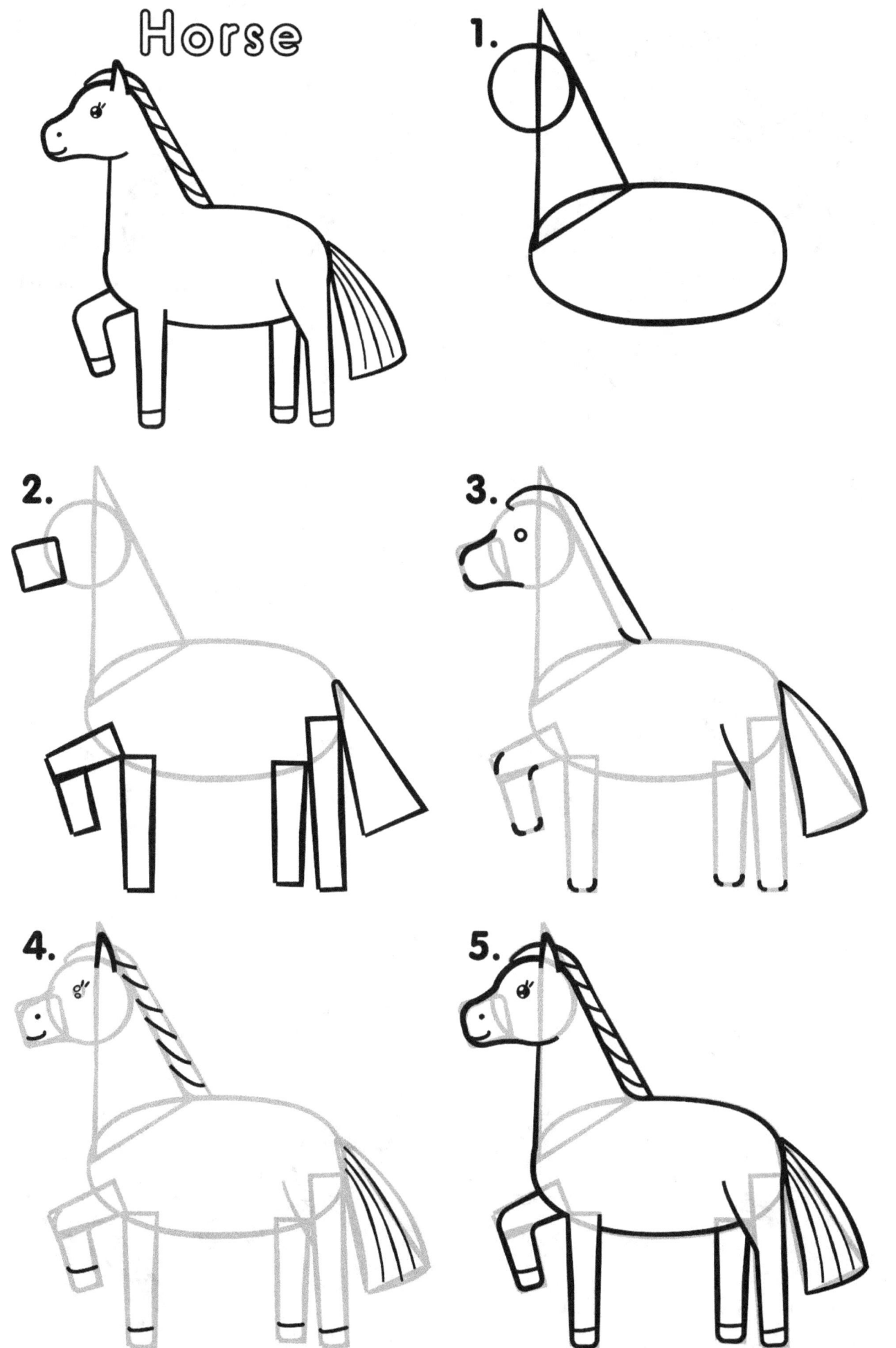

1.

2.

3.

4.

5.

Iguana

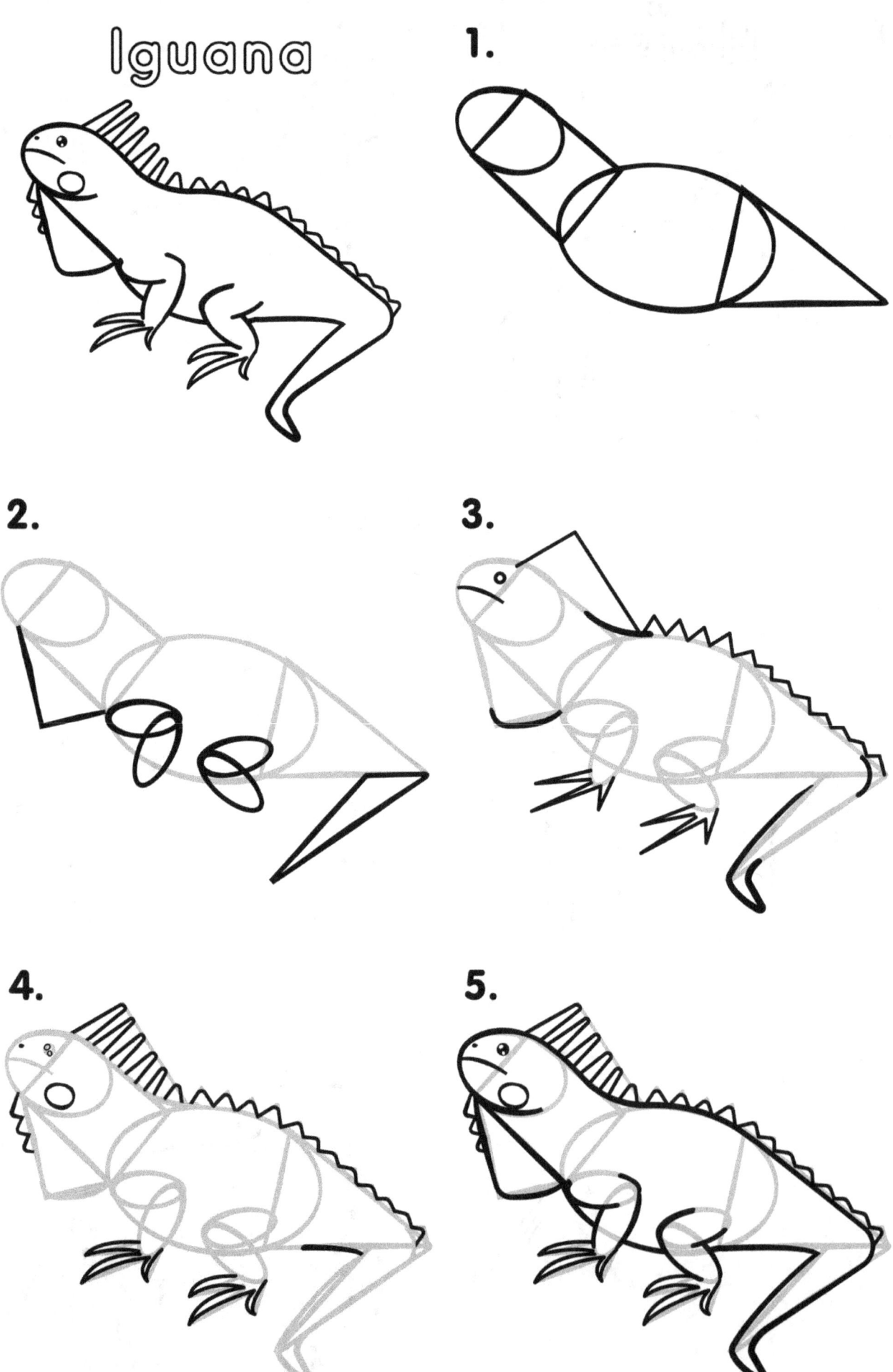

1.

2.

3.

4.

5.

Jellyfish

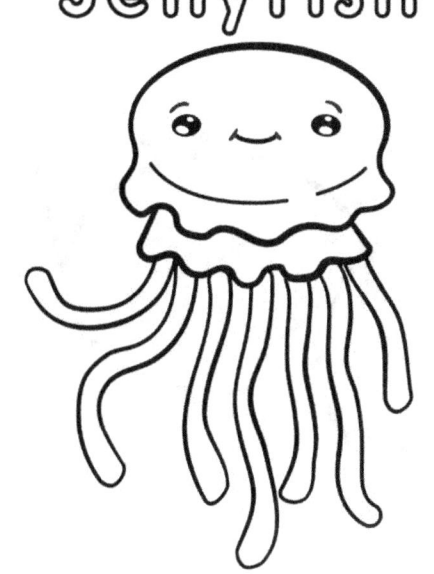

1.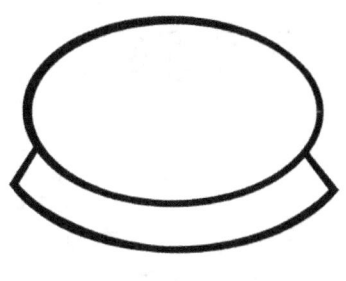

2.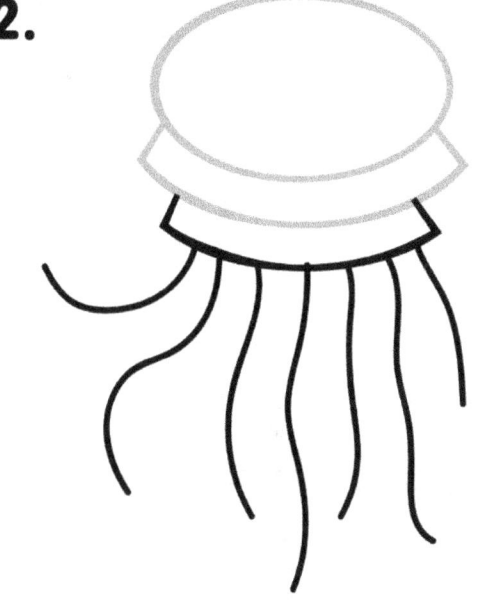

3.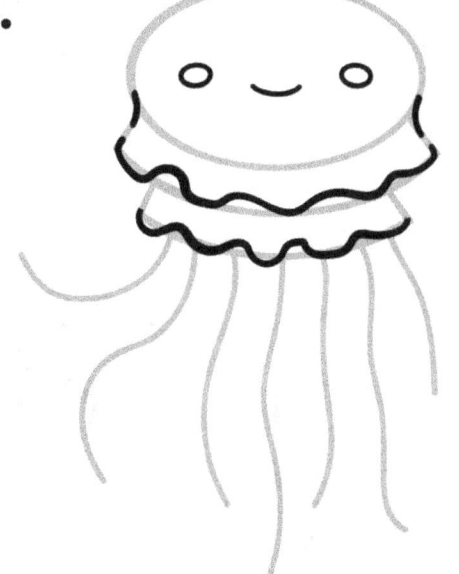

4.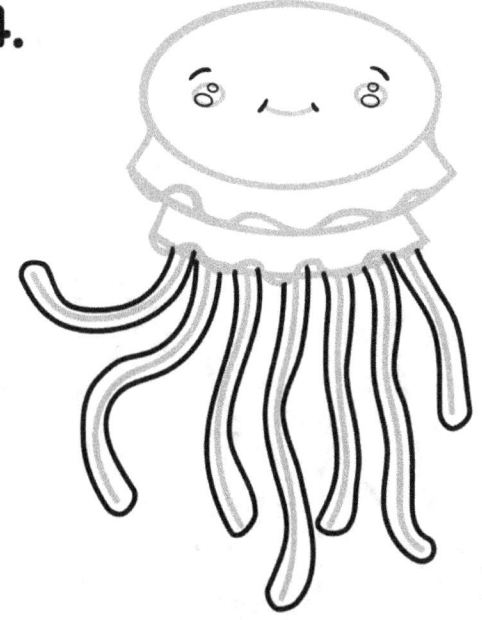

5.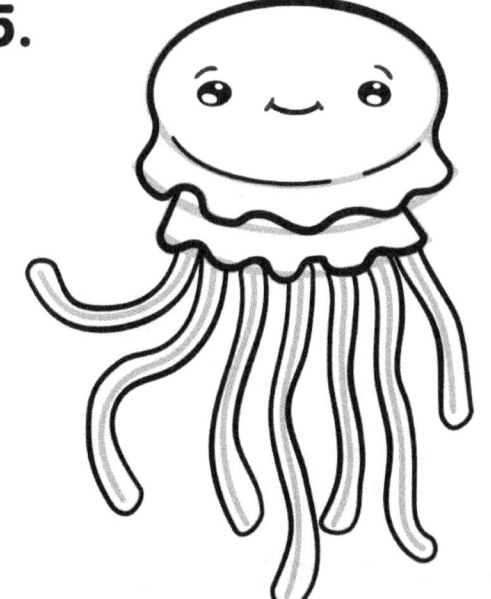

Kangaroo

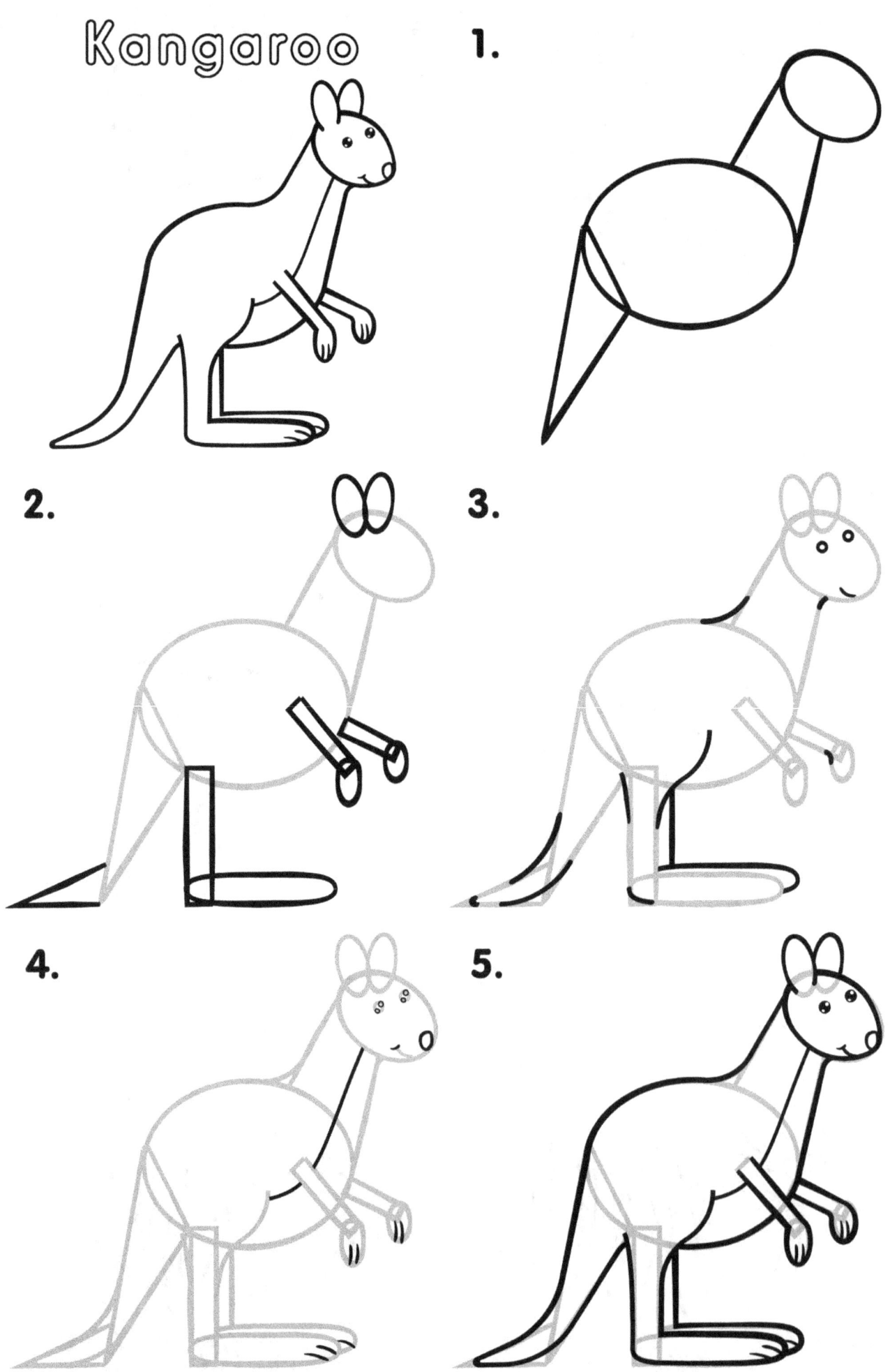

1.

2.

3.

4.

5.

Lion

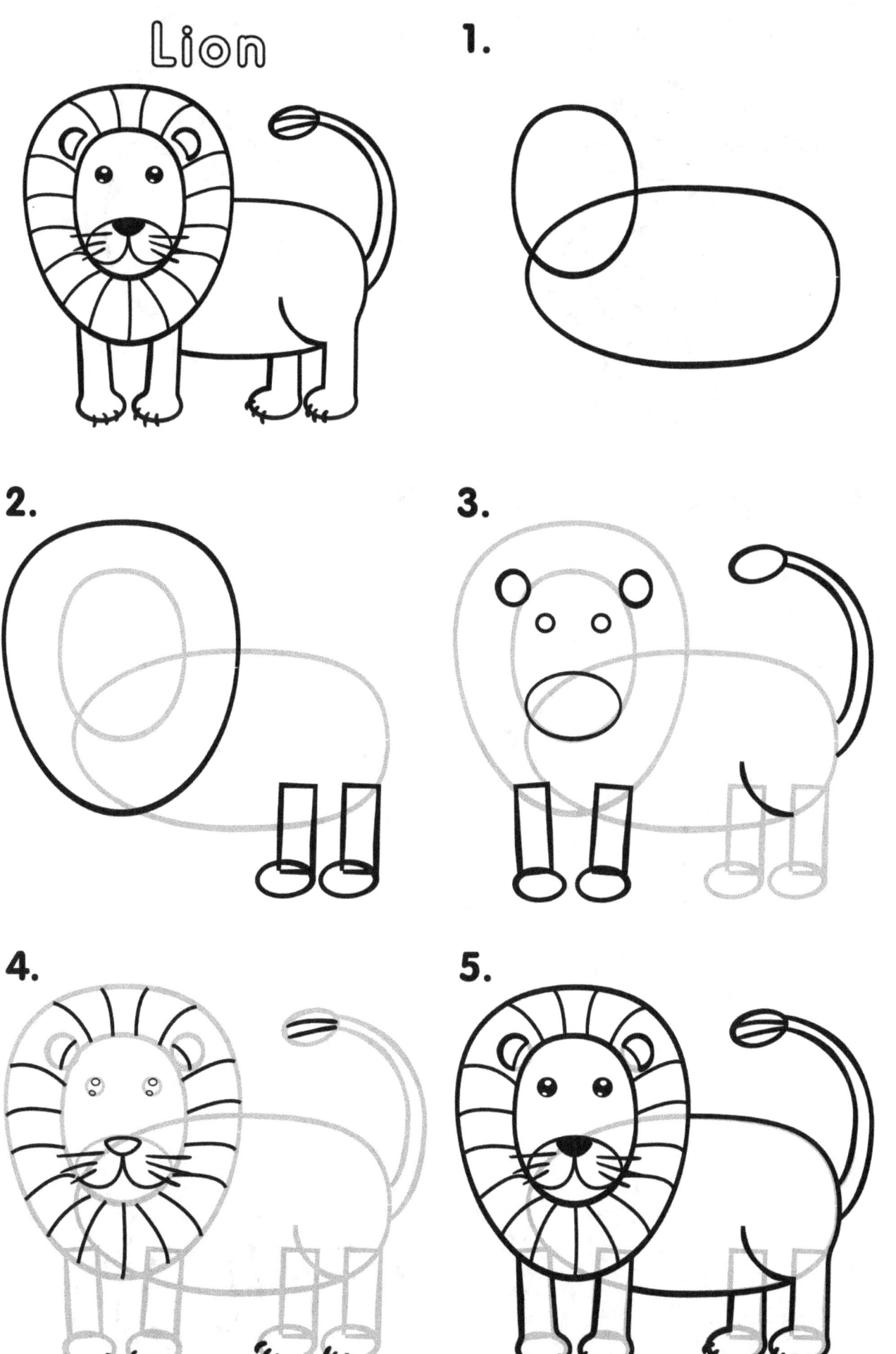

1.

2.

3.

4.

5.

Monkey

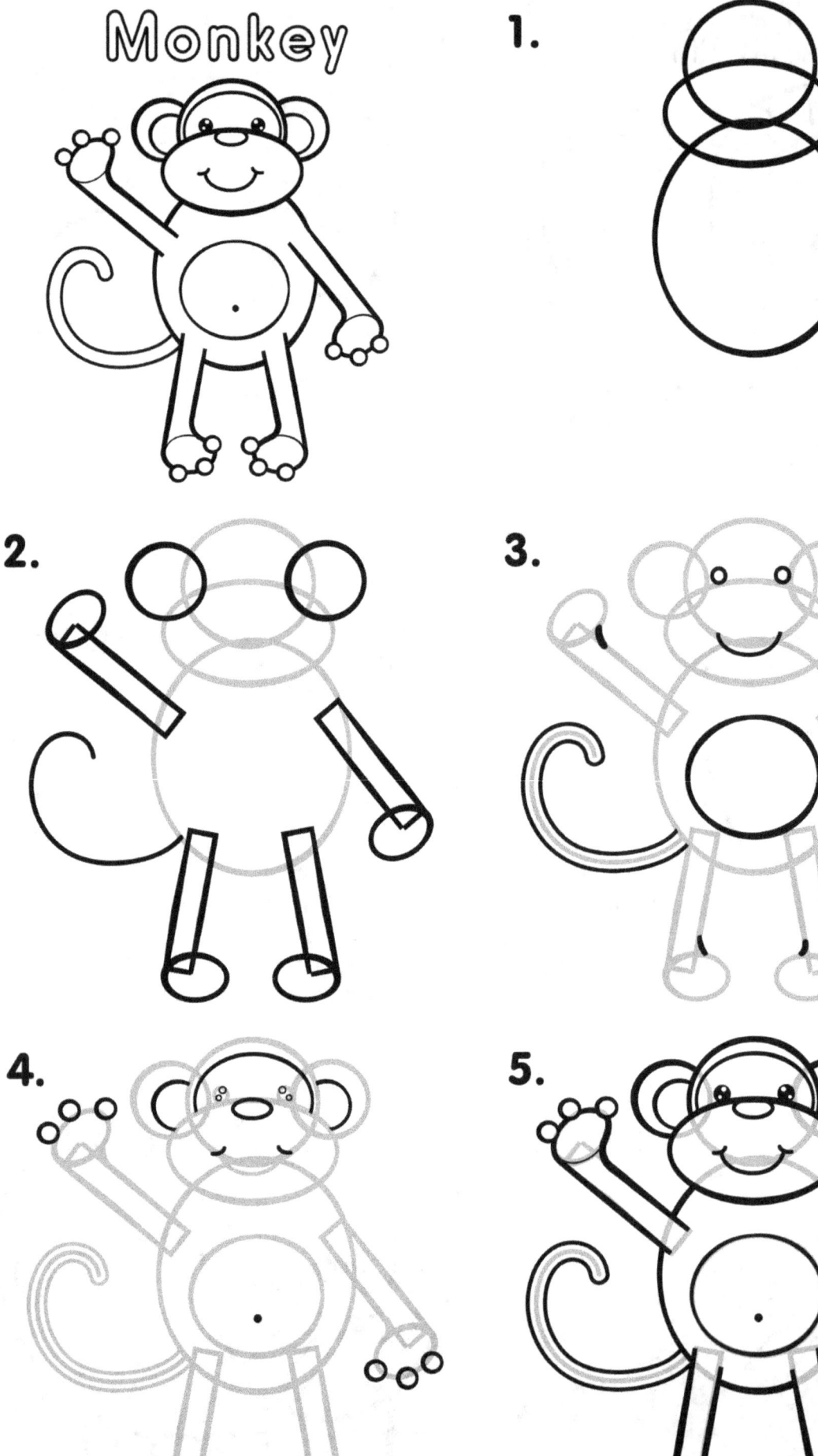

1.

2.

3.

4.

5.

Nightingale

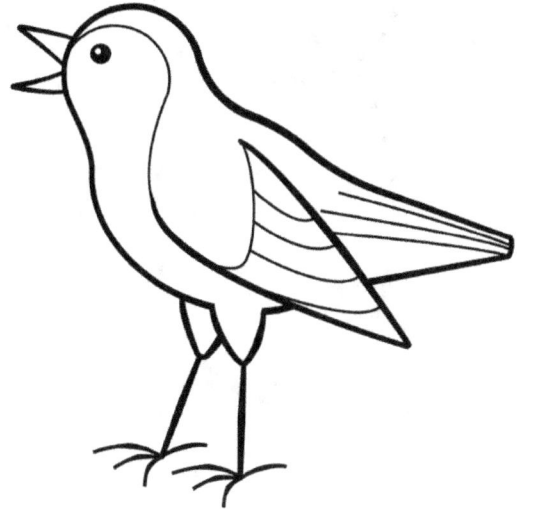

1.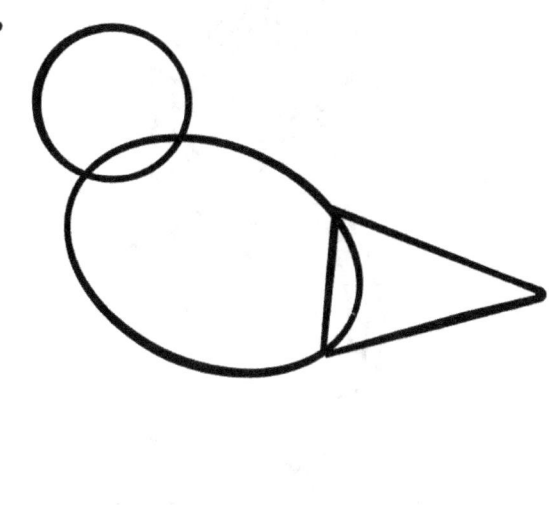

2.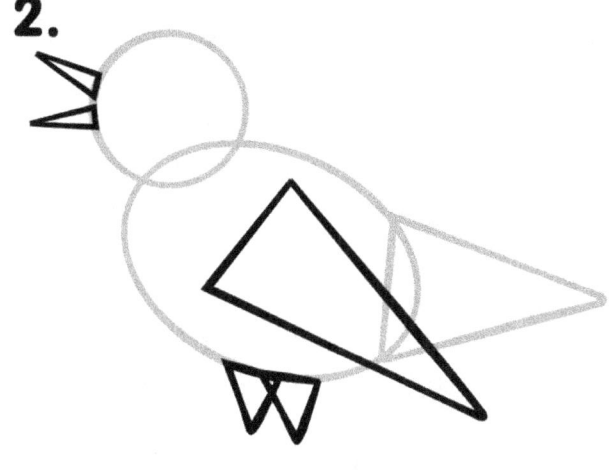

3.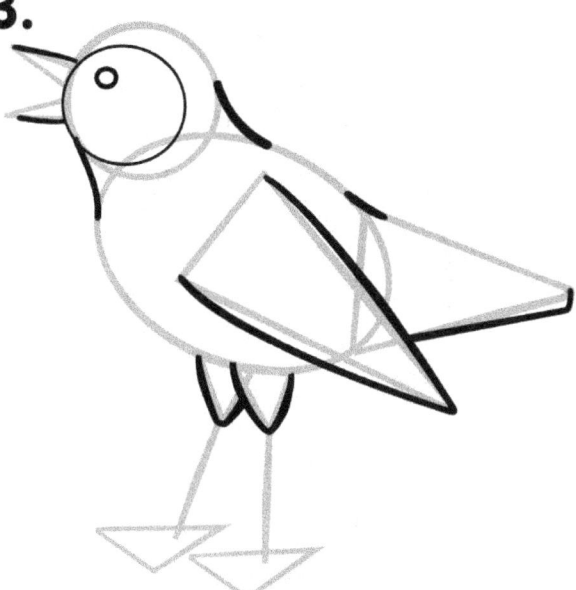

4.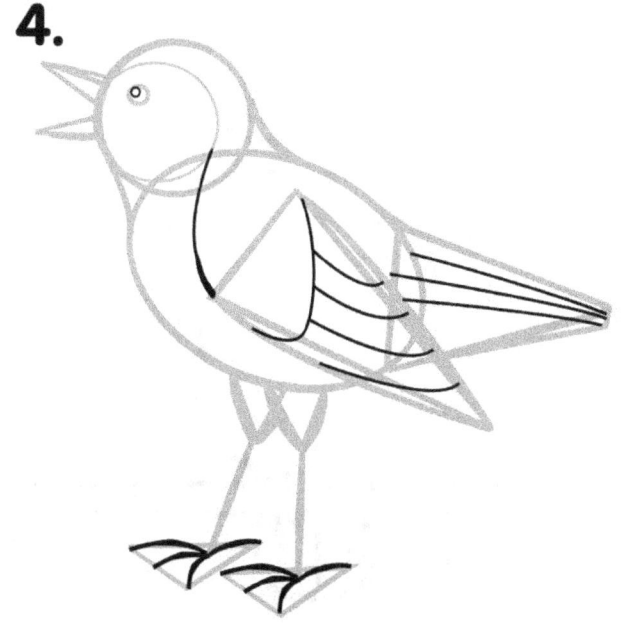

5.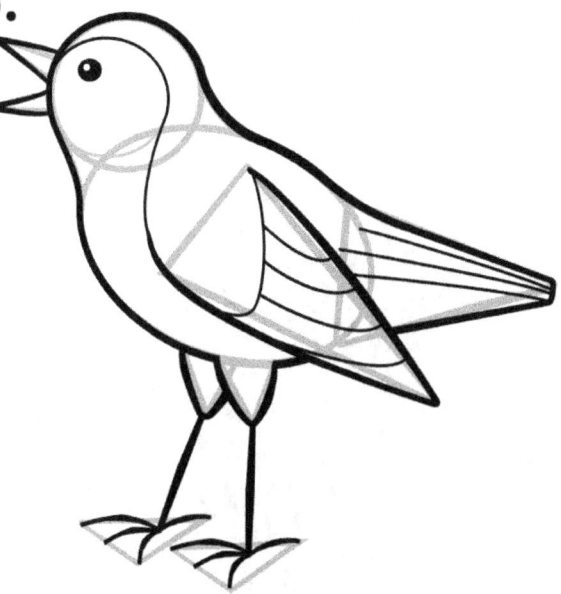

Owl

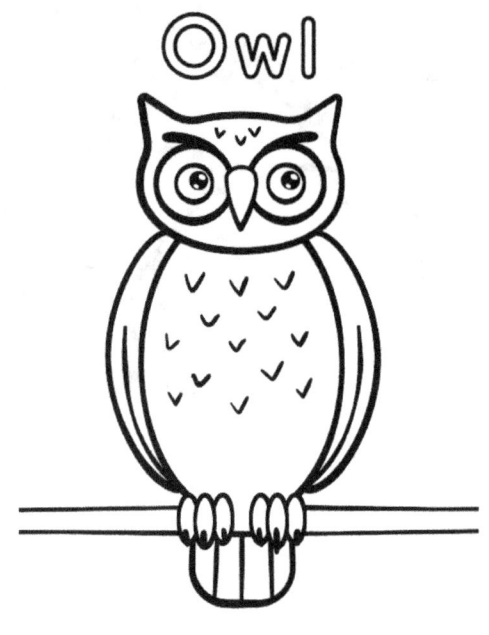

1.

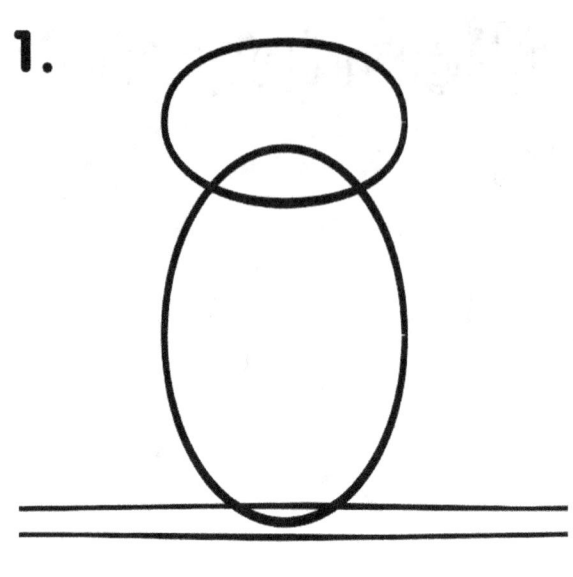

2.

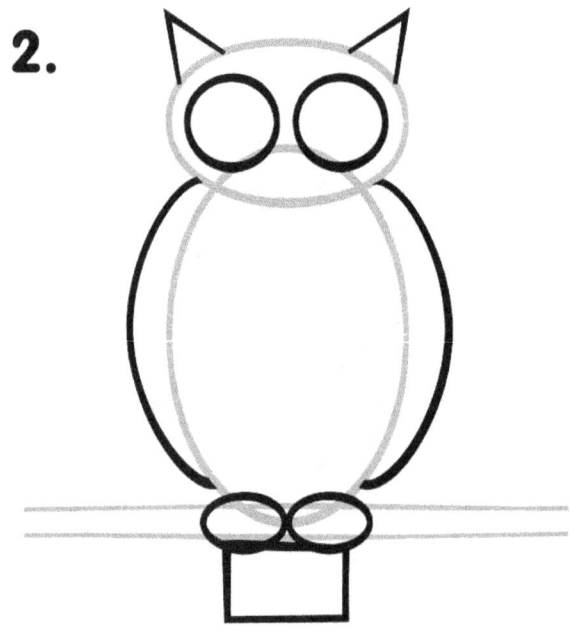

3.

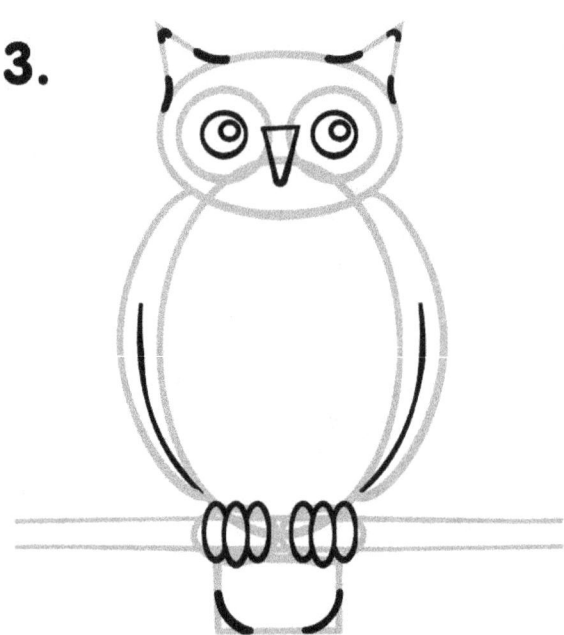

4.

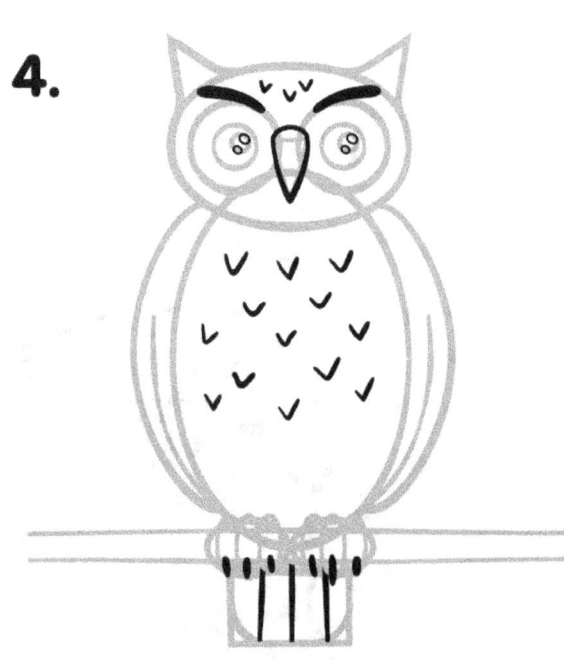

5.

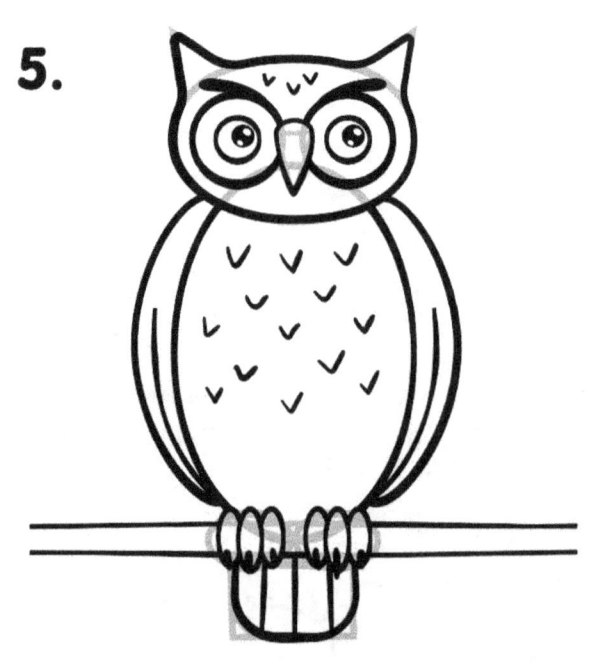

Pig

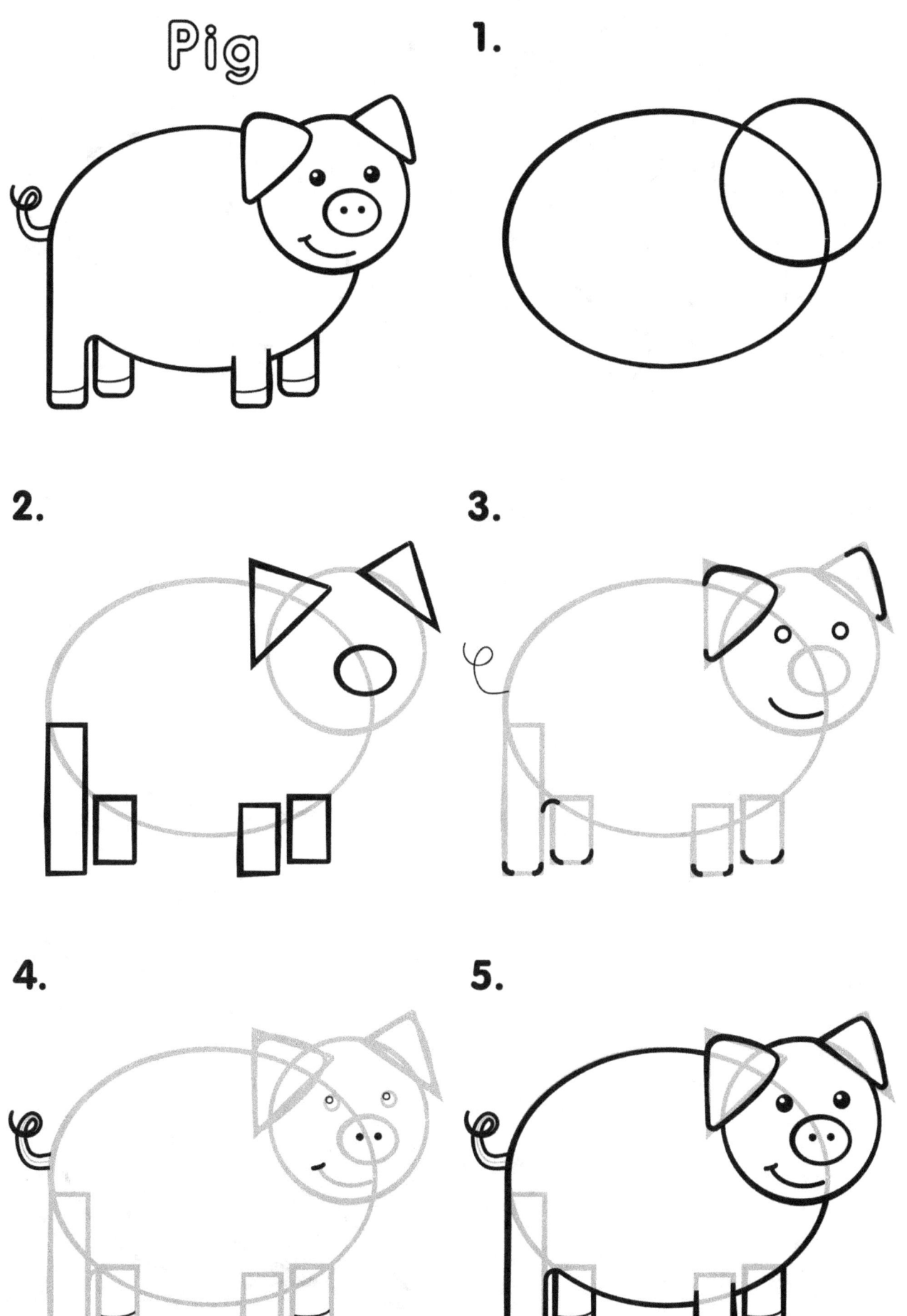

1.

2.

3.

4.

5.

Quail

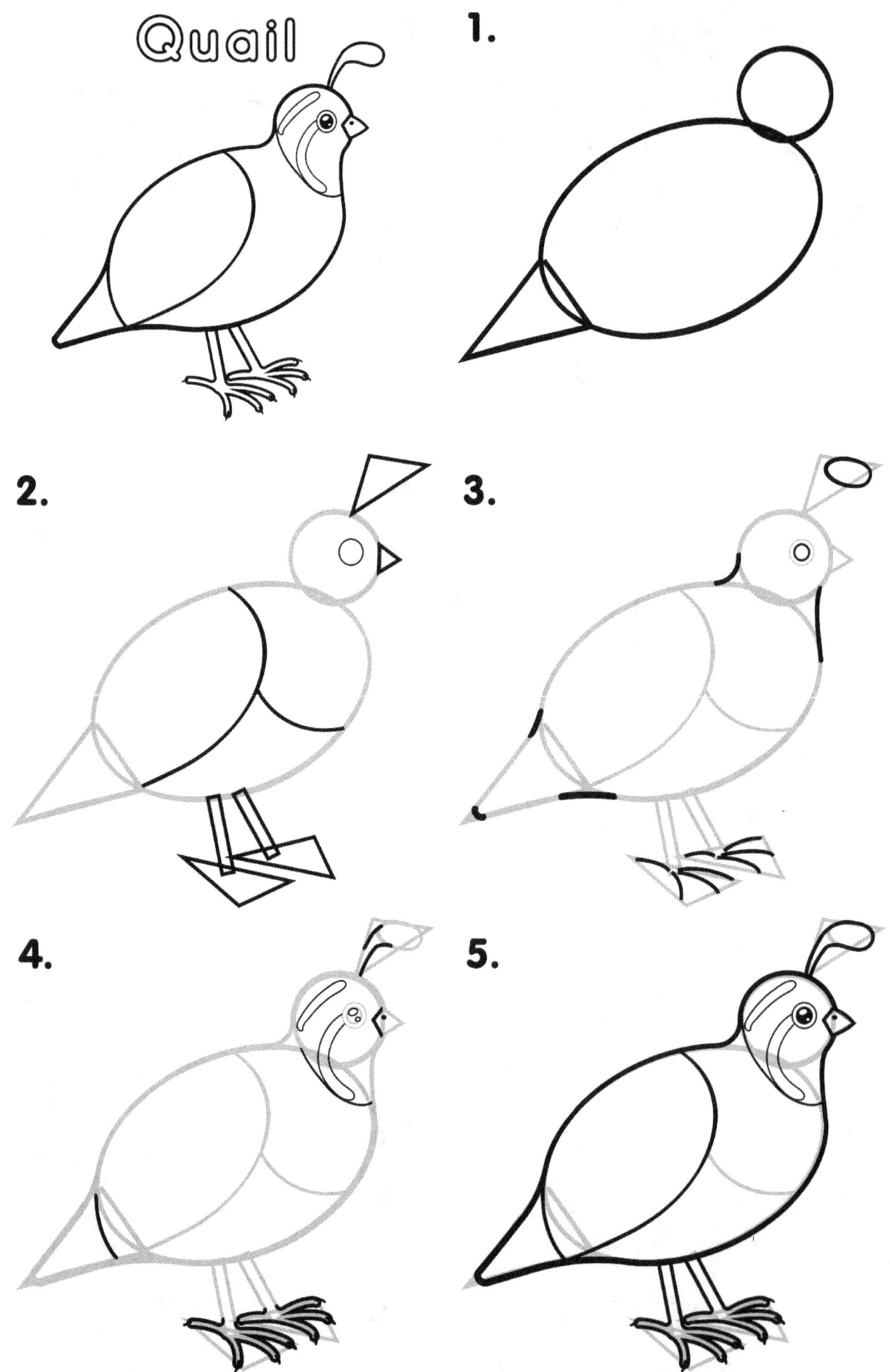

Rabbit

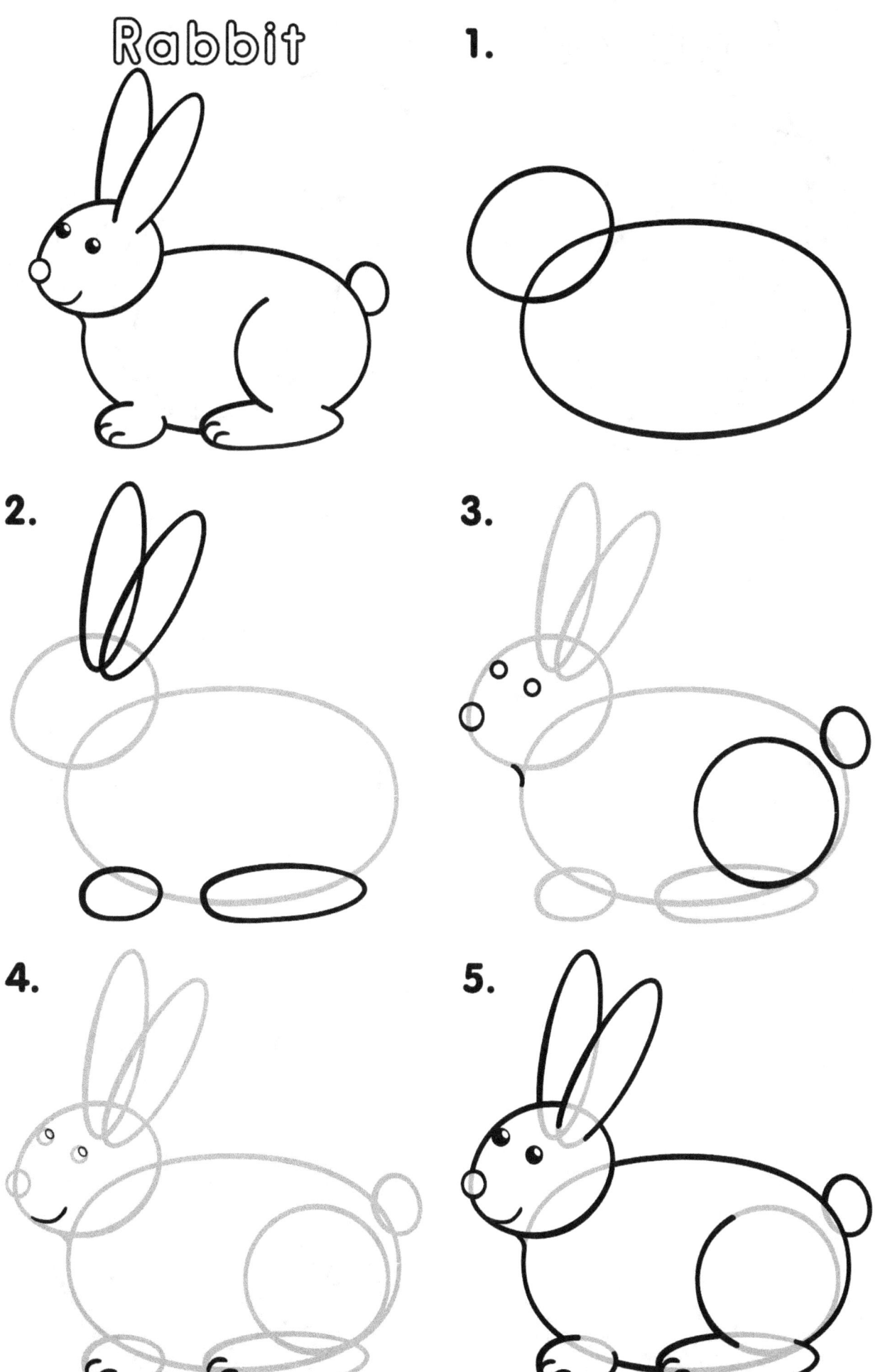

1.

2.

3.

4.

5.

Squirrel

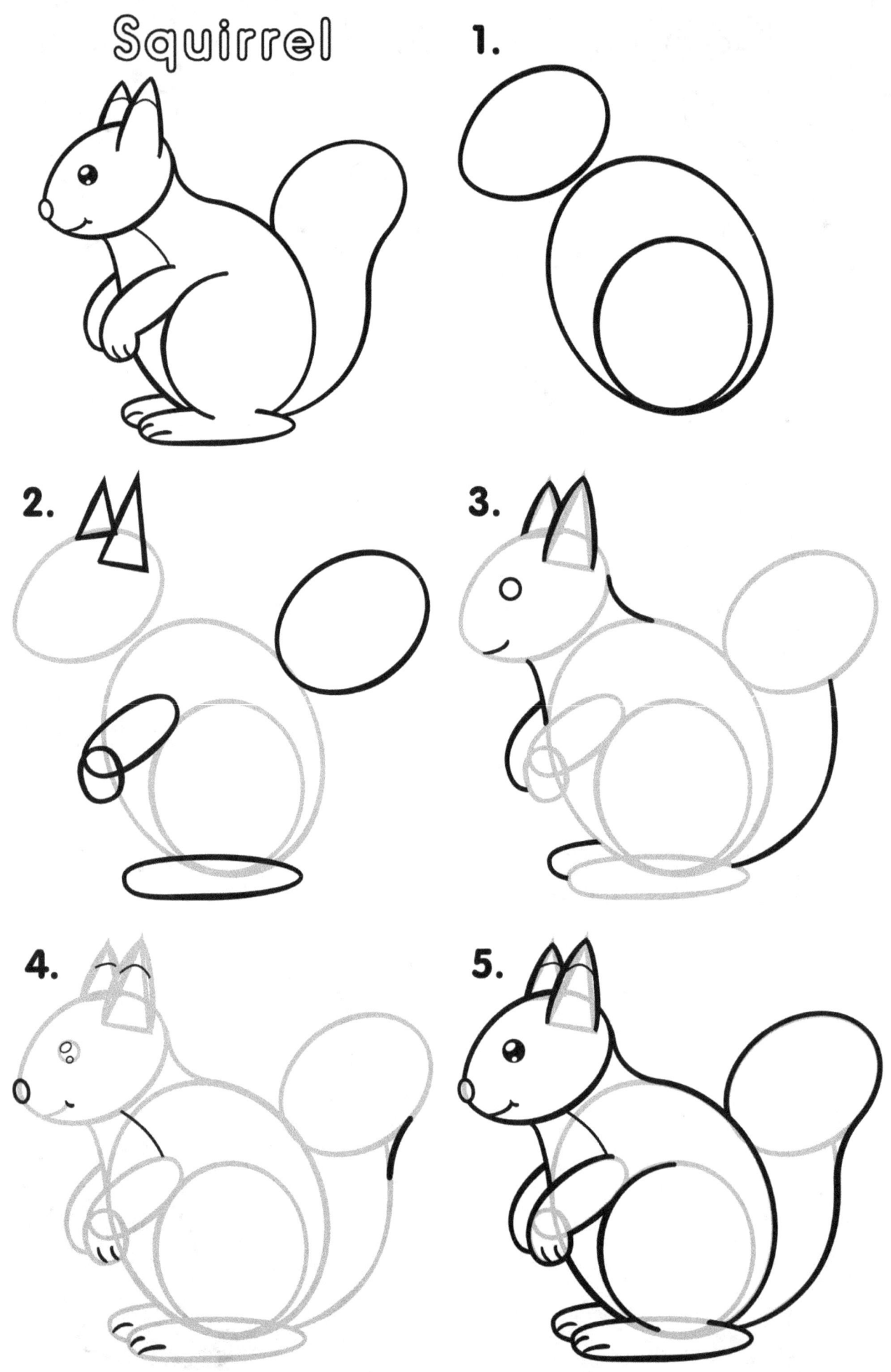

1.

2.

3.

4.

5.

Turtle

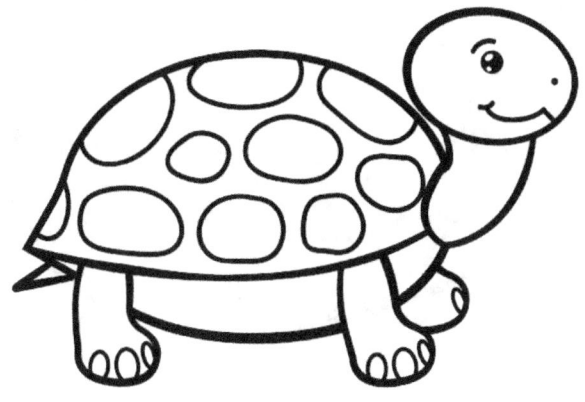

1.

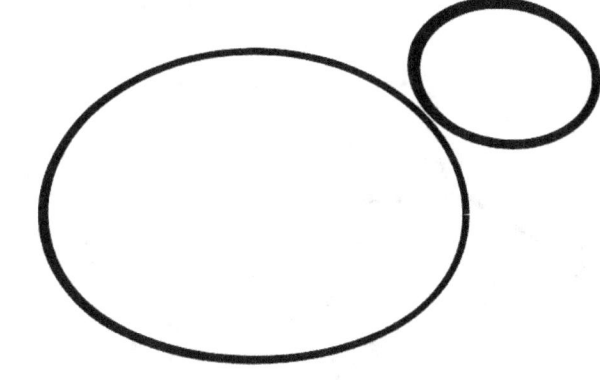

2.

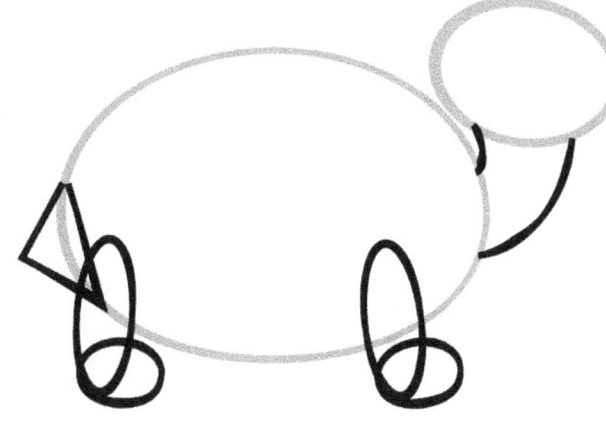

3.

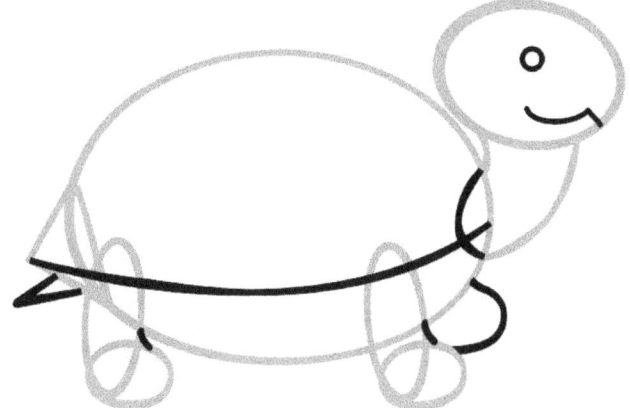

4.

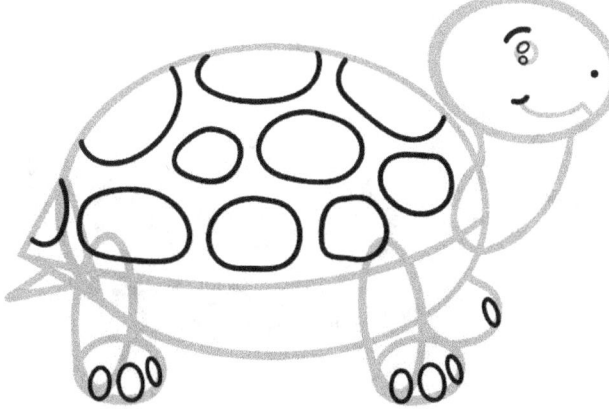

5.

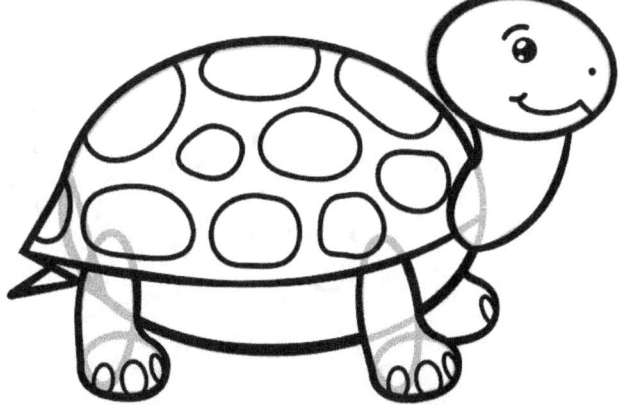

Urchin

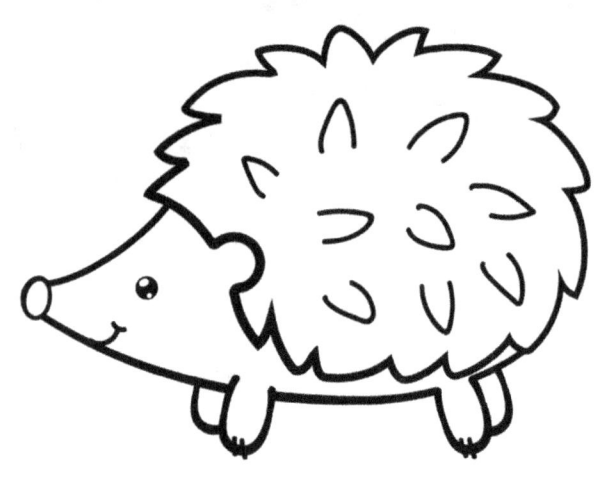

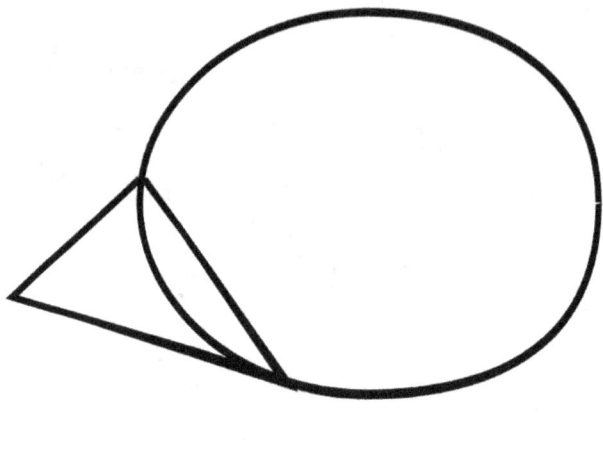

2.

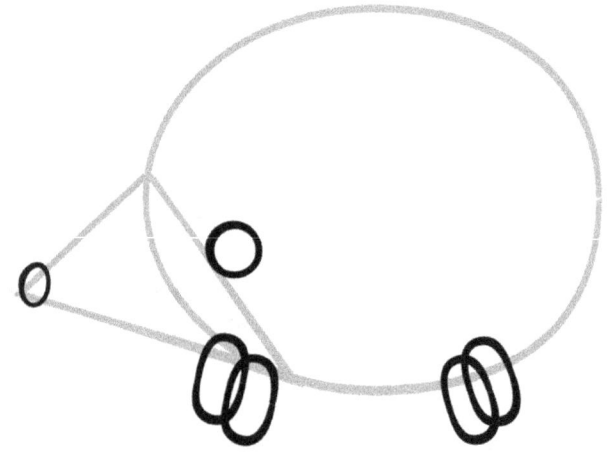

3.

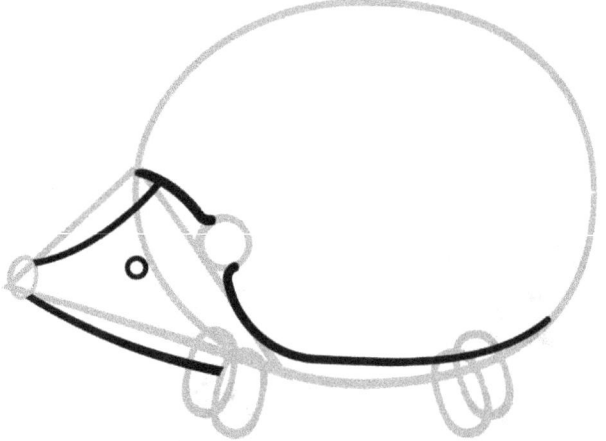

4.

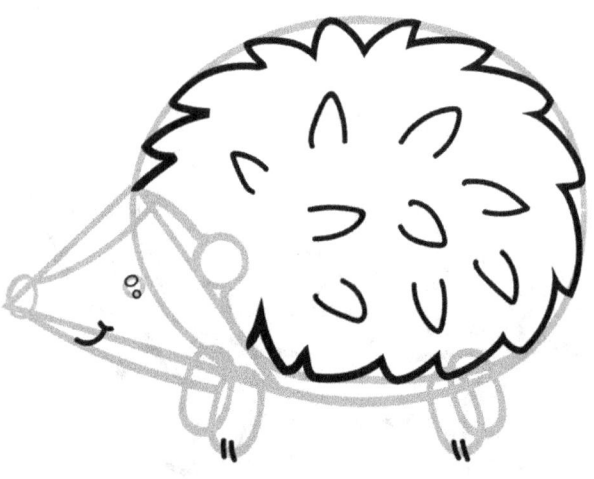

5.

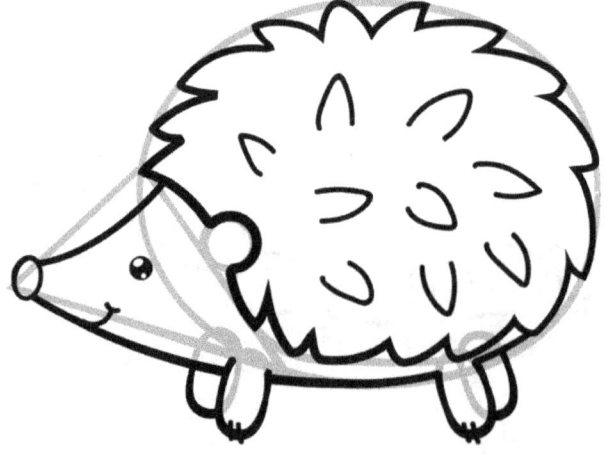

Viper

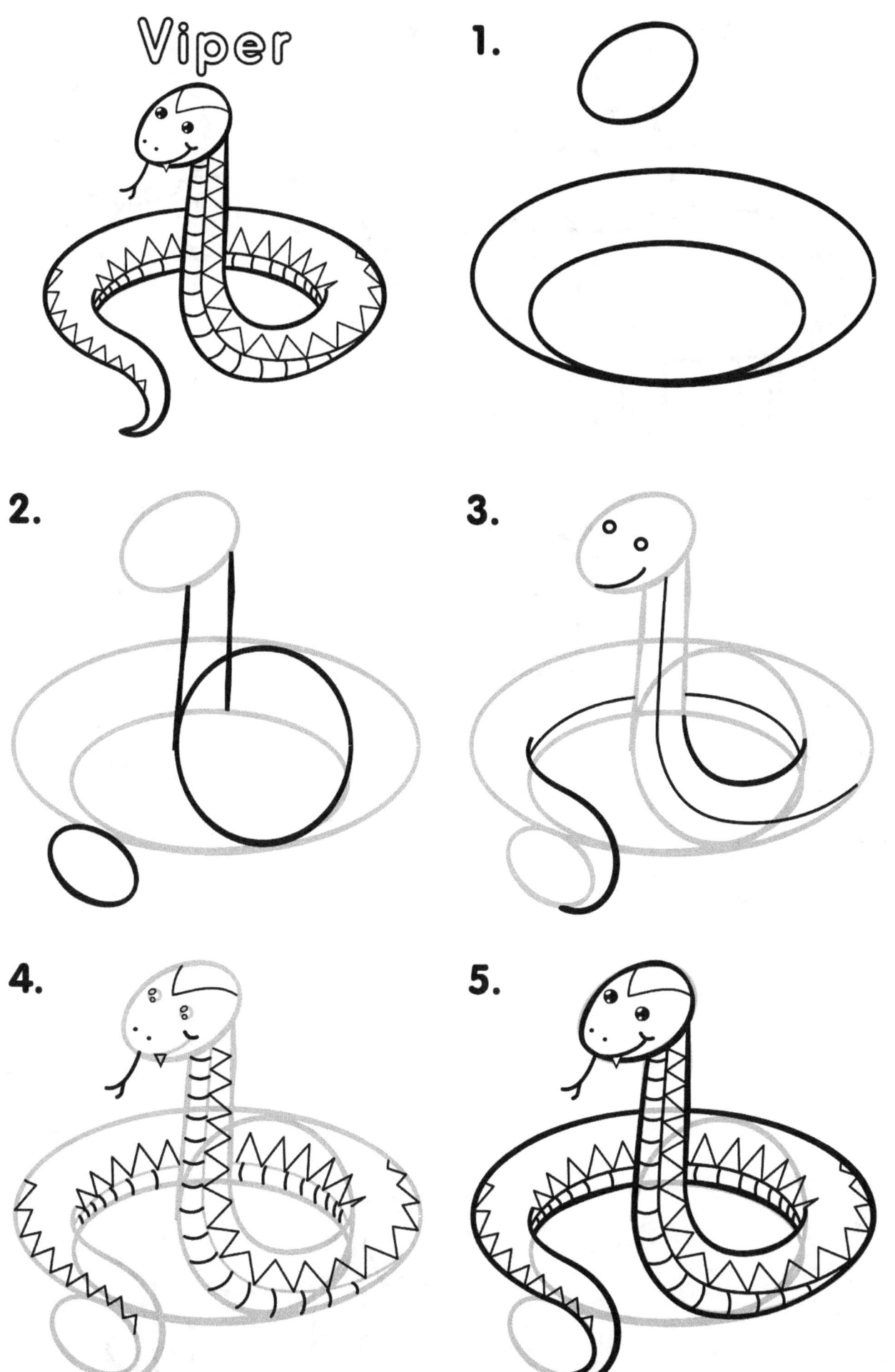

1.

2.

3.

4.

5.

Wolf

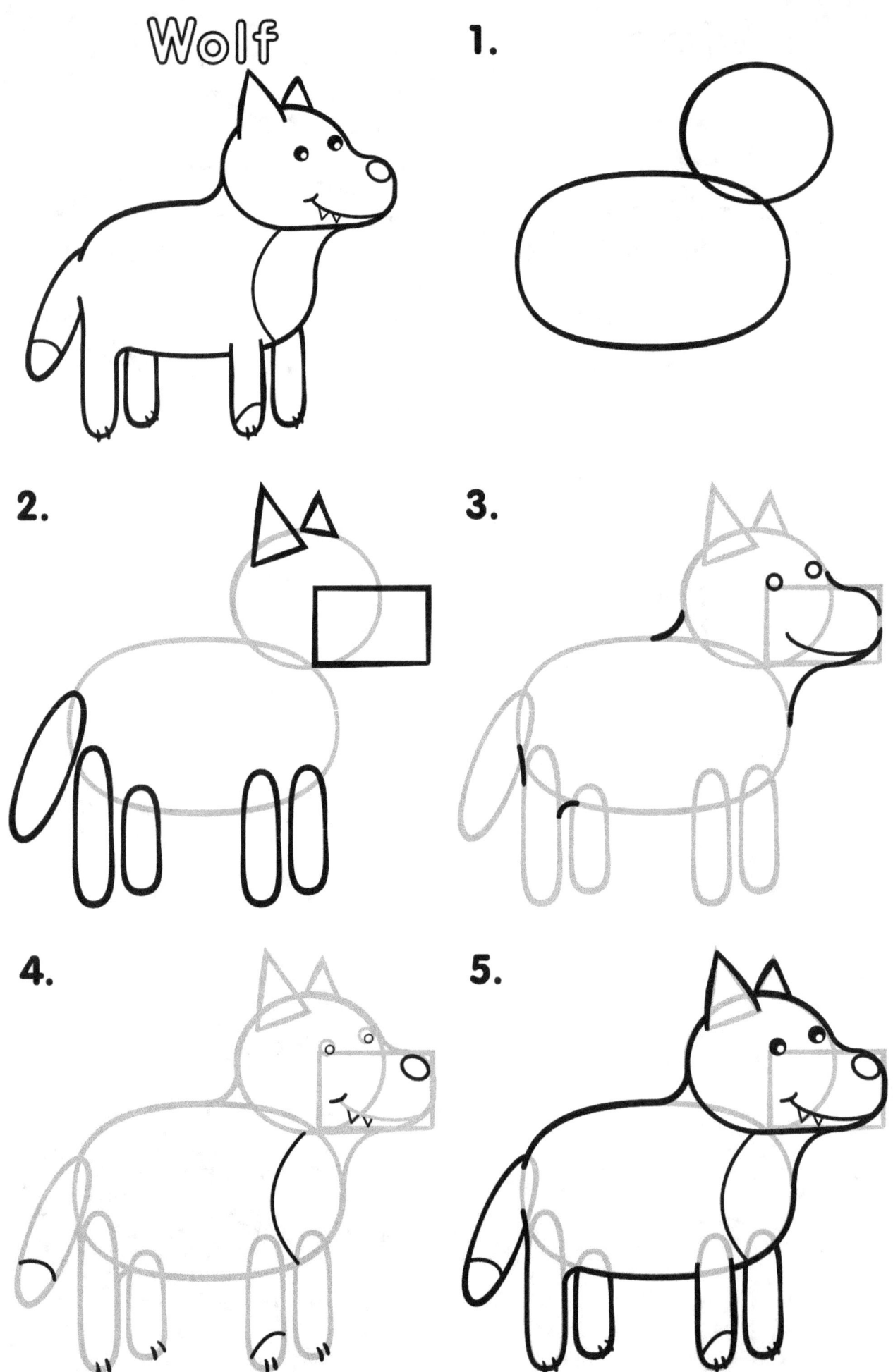

1.

2.

3.

4.

5.

X-Ray Fish

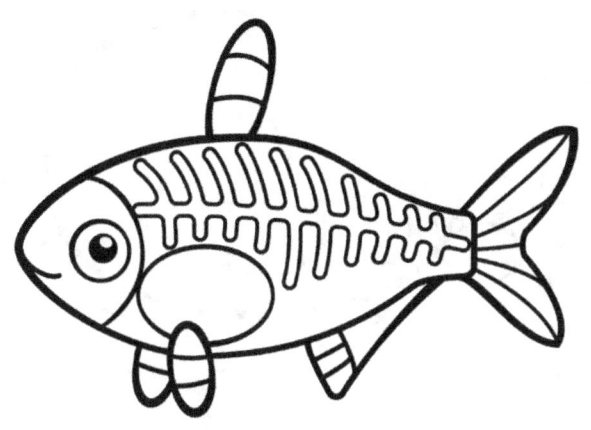

1.

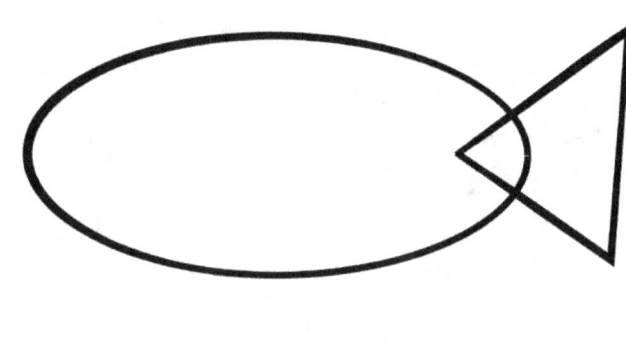

2.

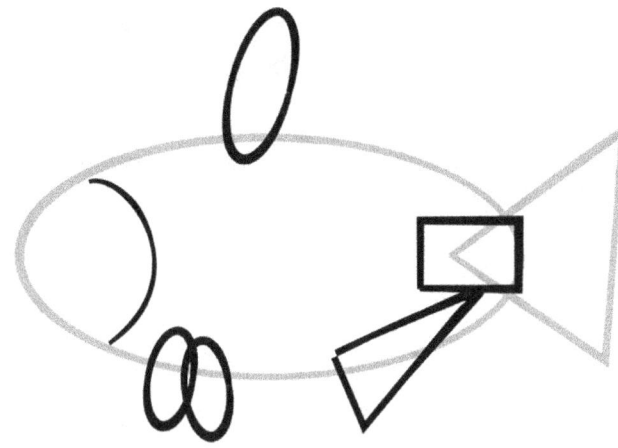

3.

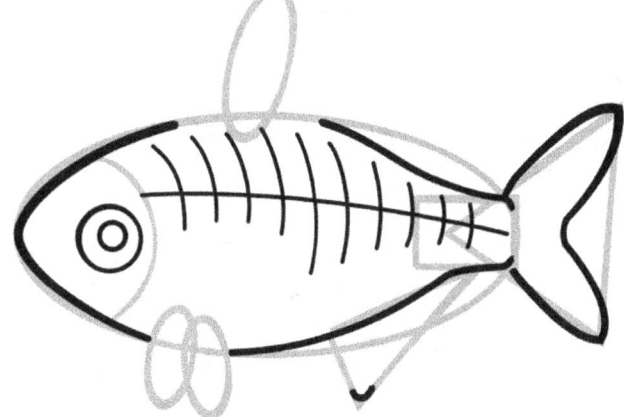

4.

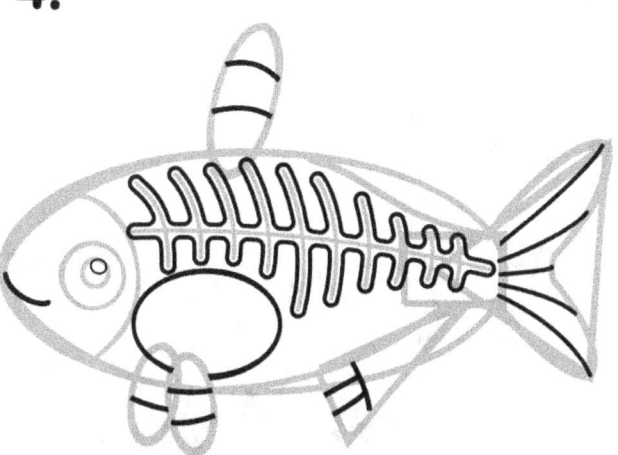

5.

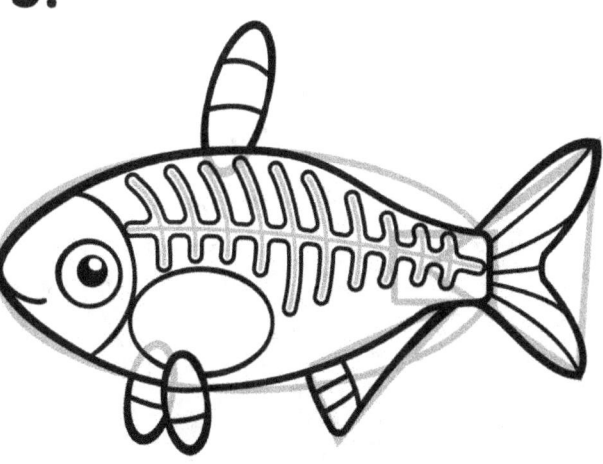

Yak

1.

2.

3.

4.

5.

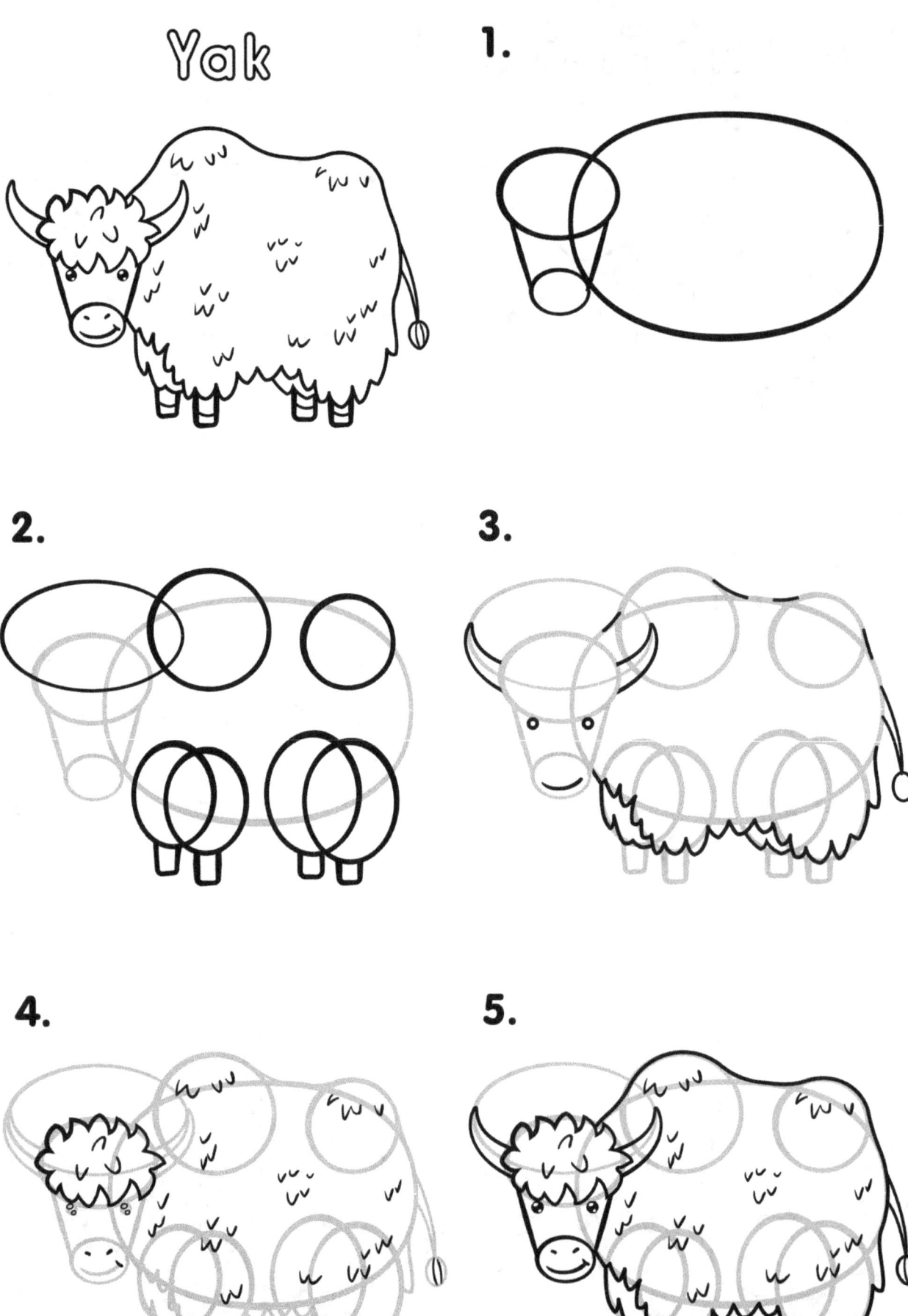

Zebra

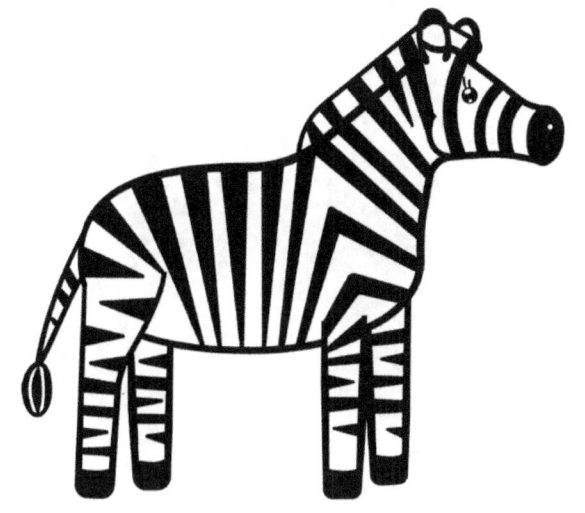

1.

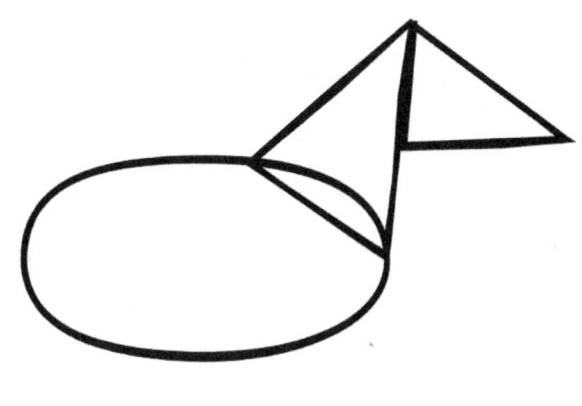

2.

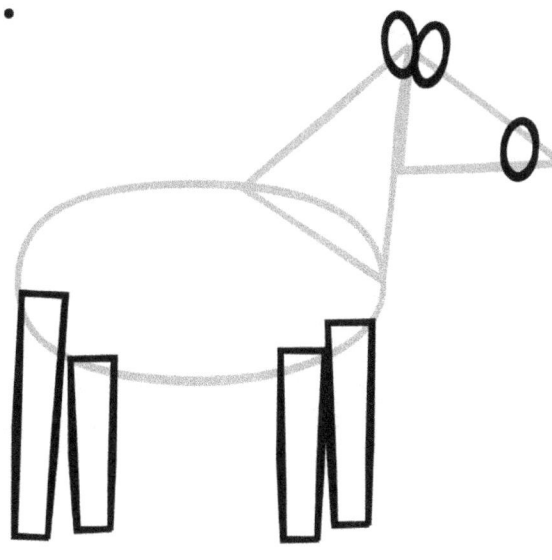

3.

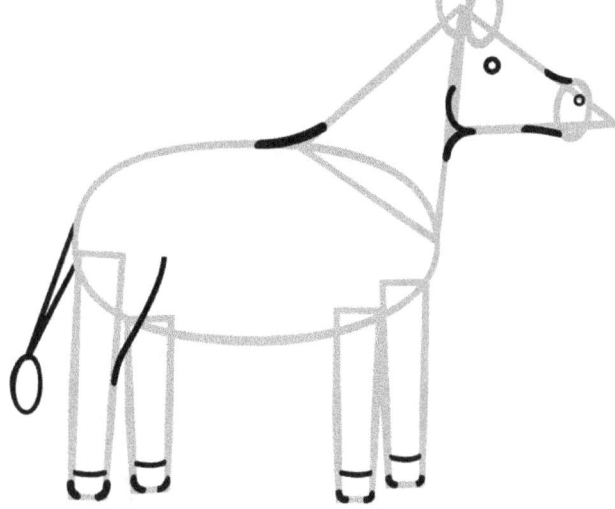

4.

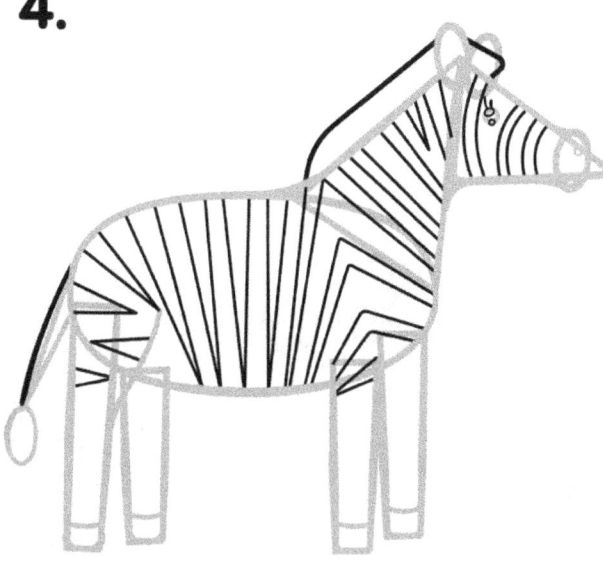

5.

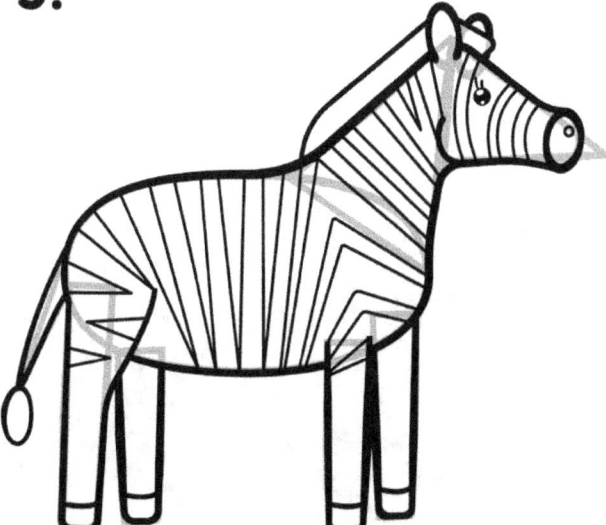

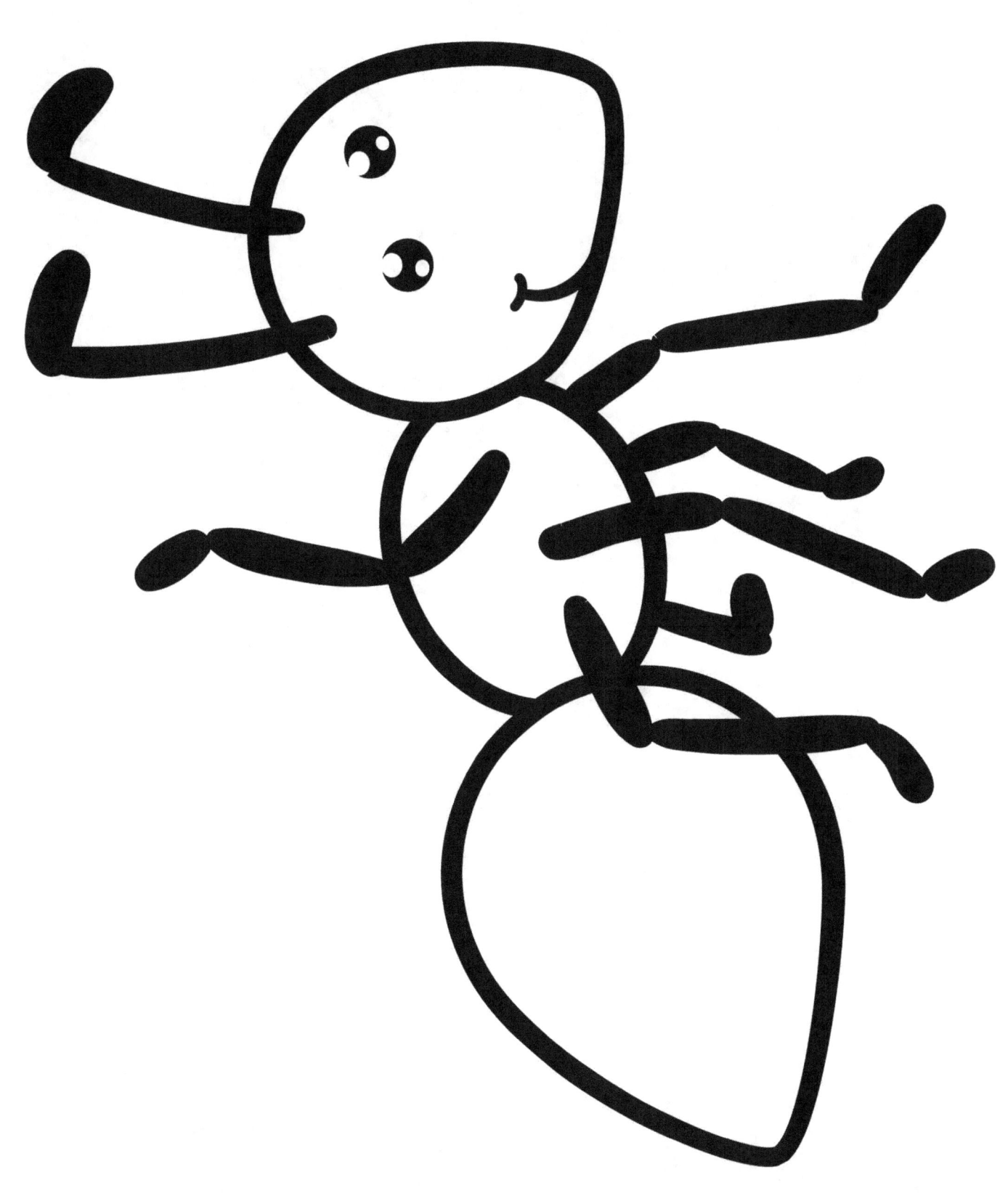

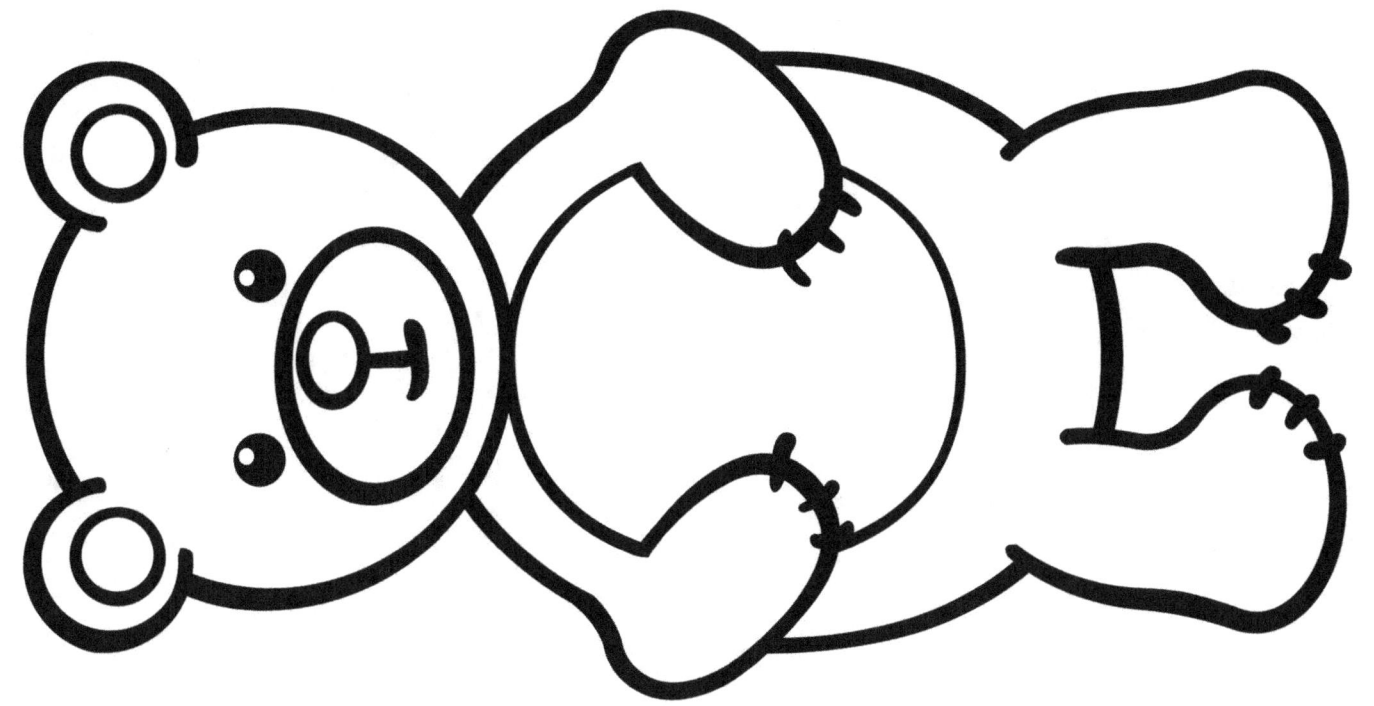

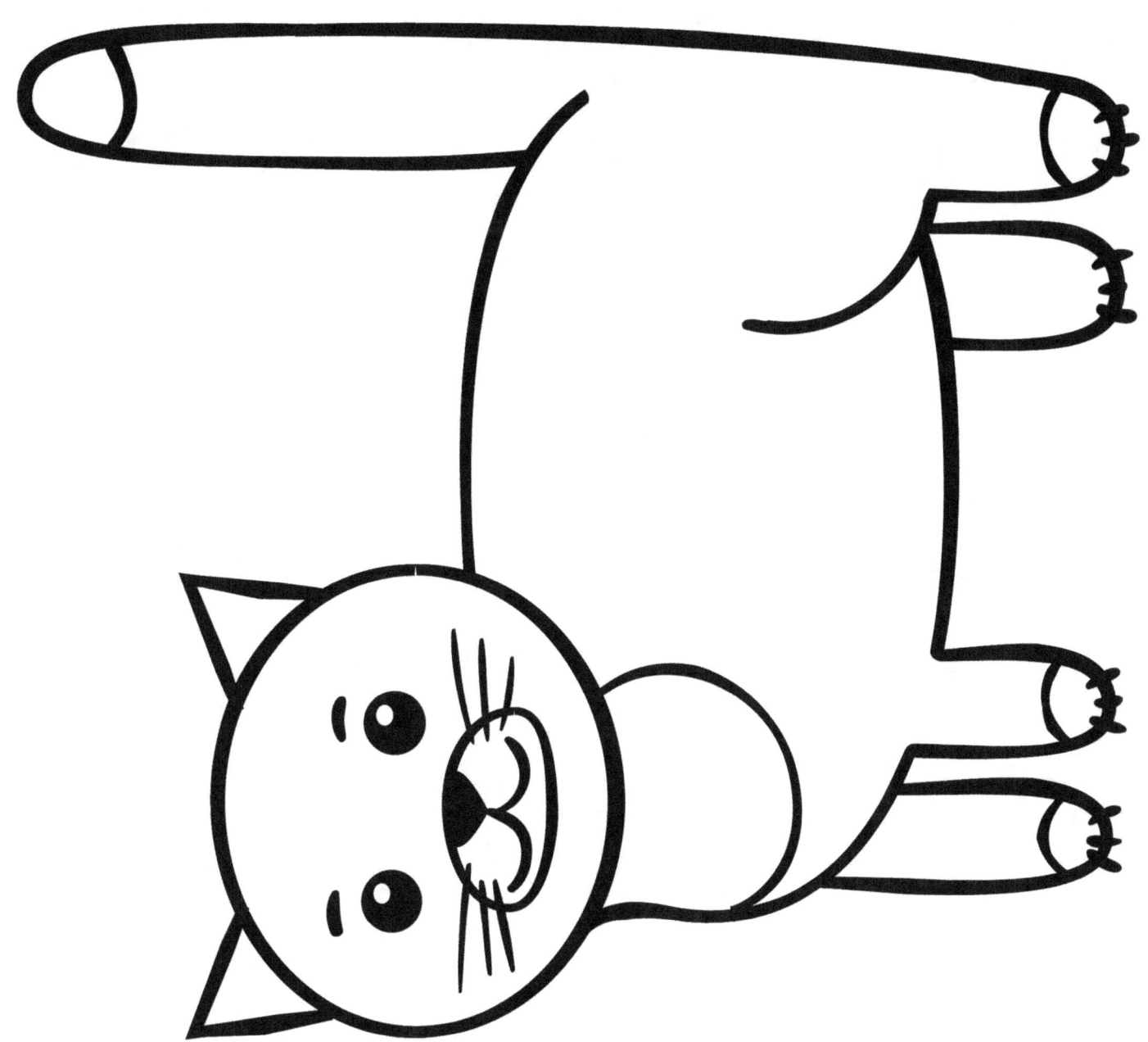

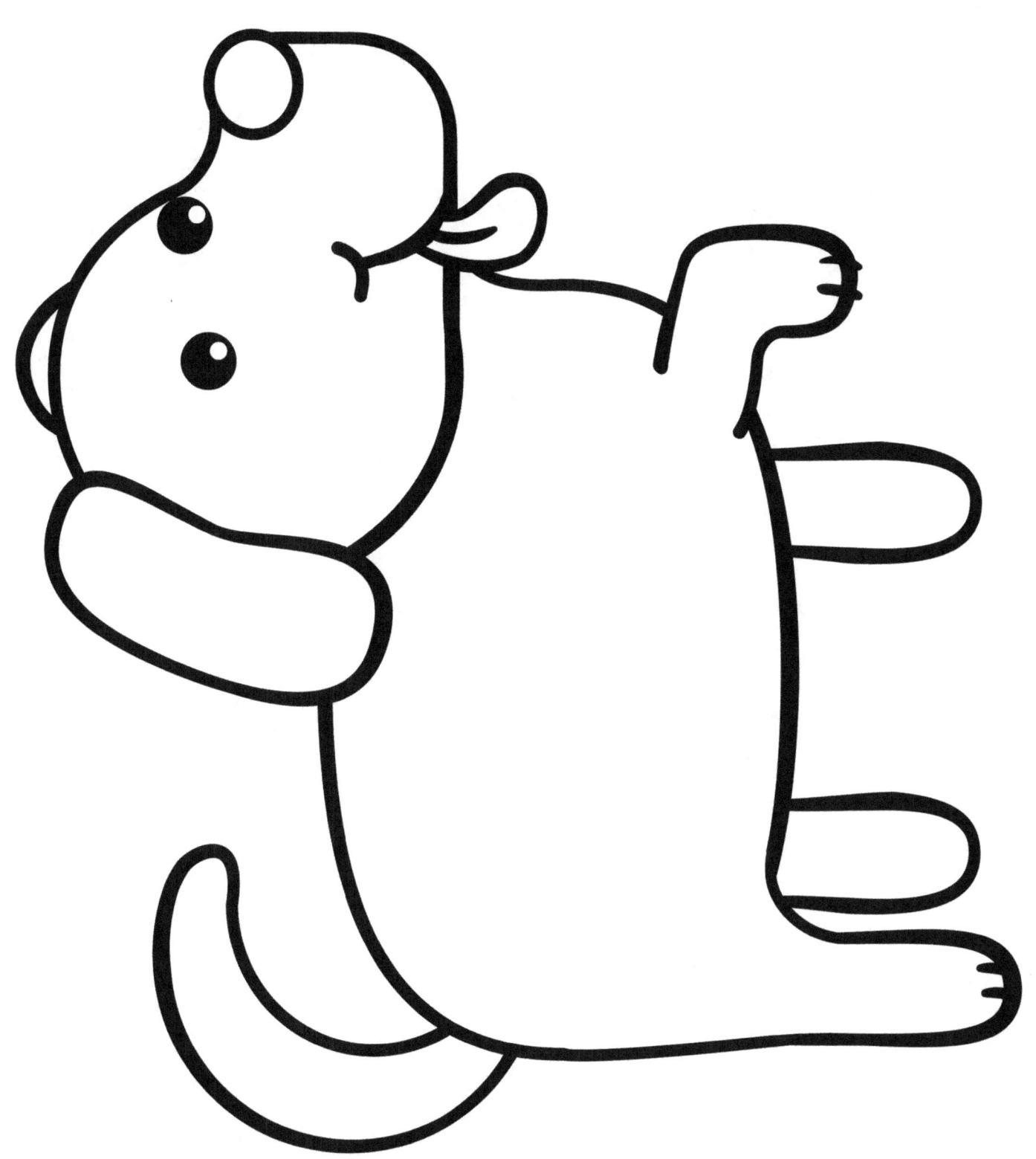

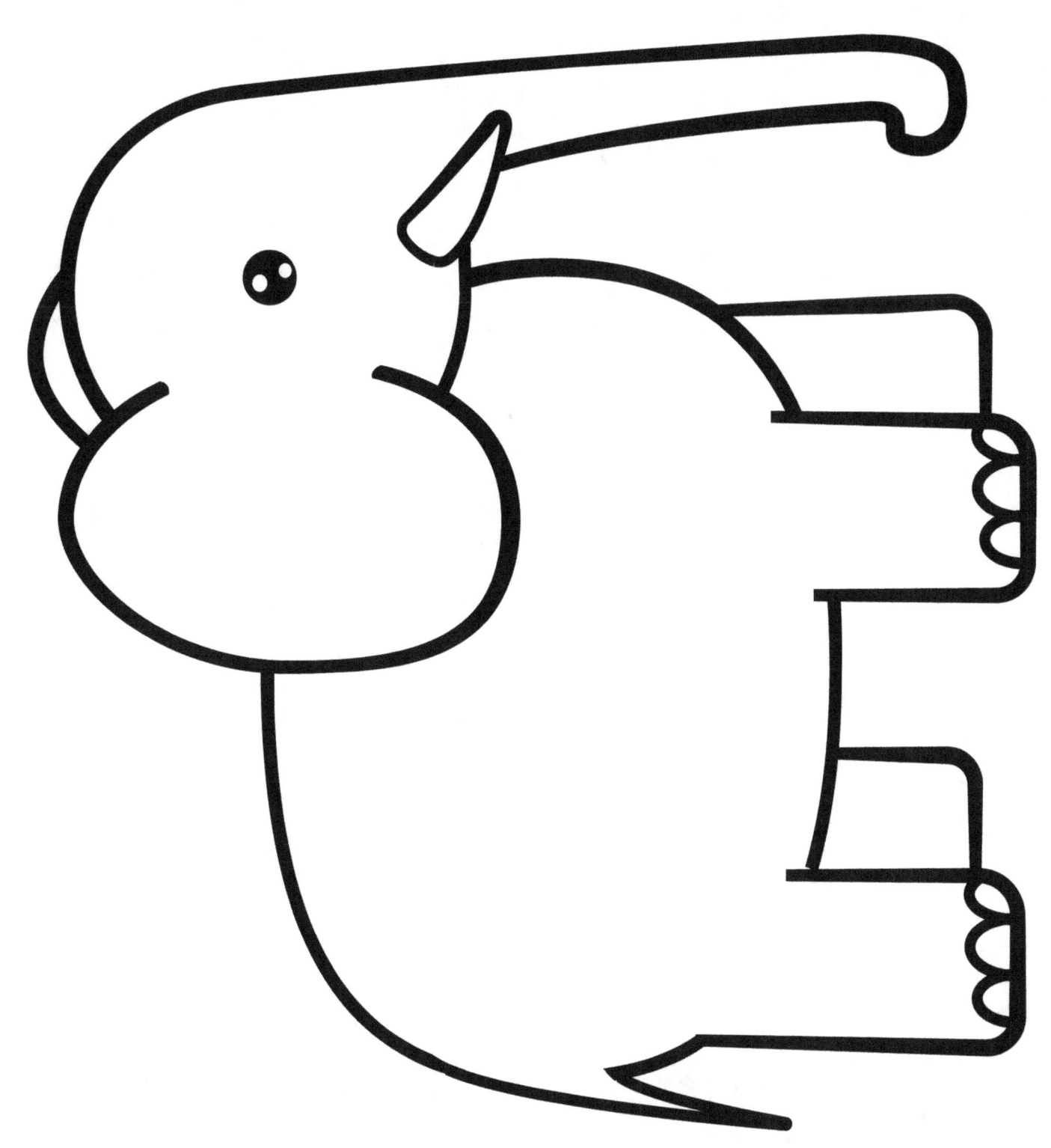

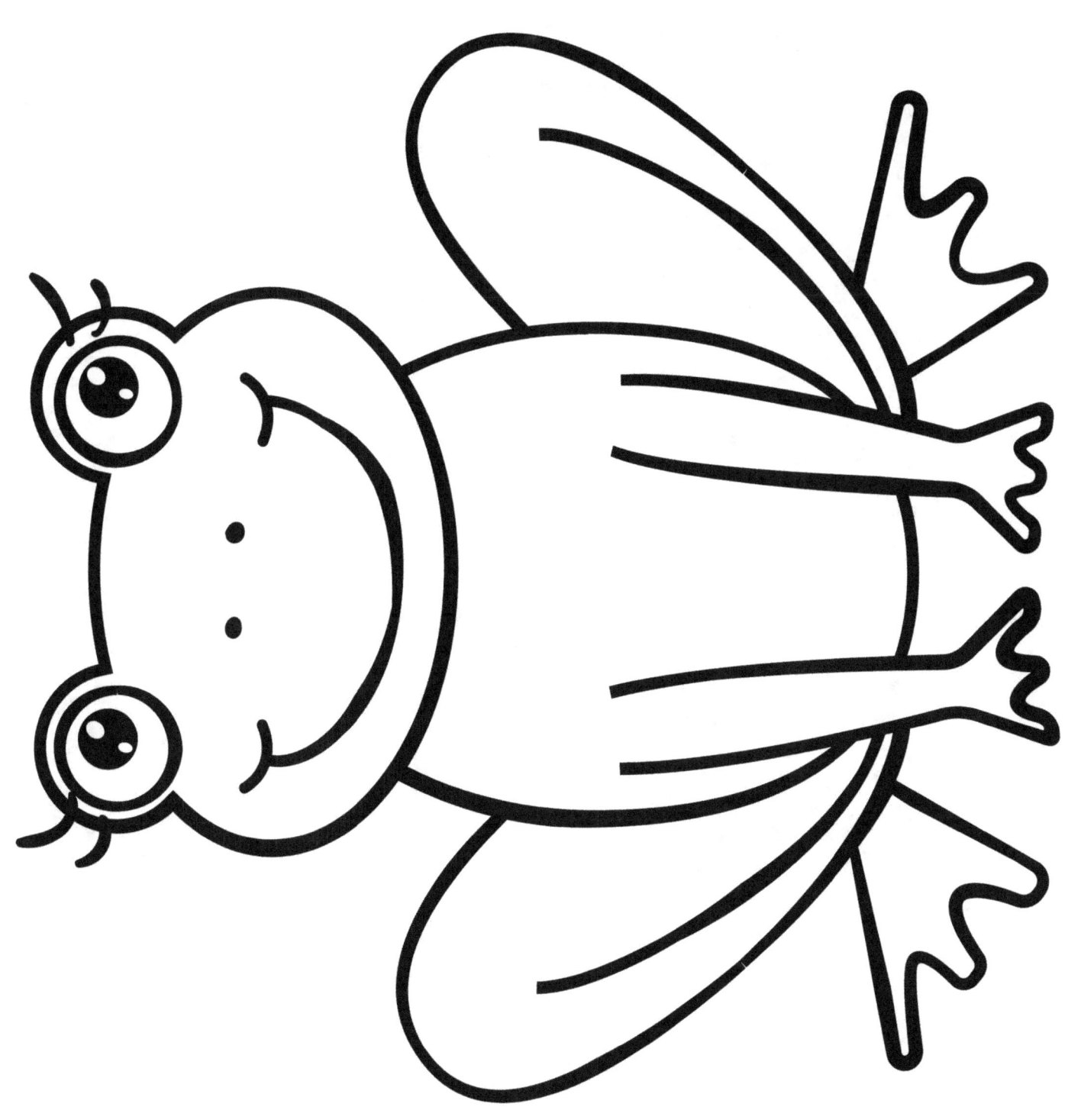

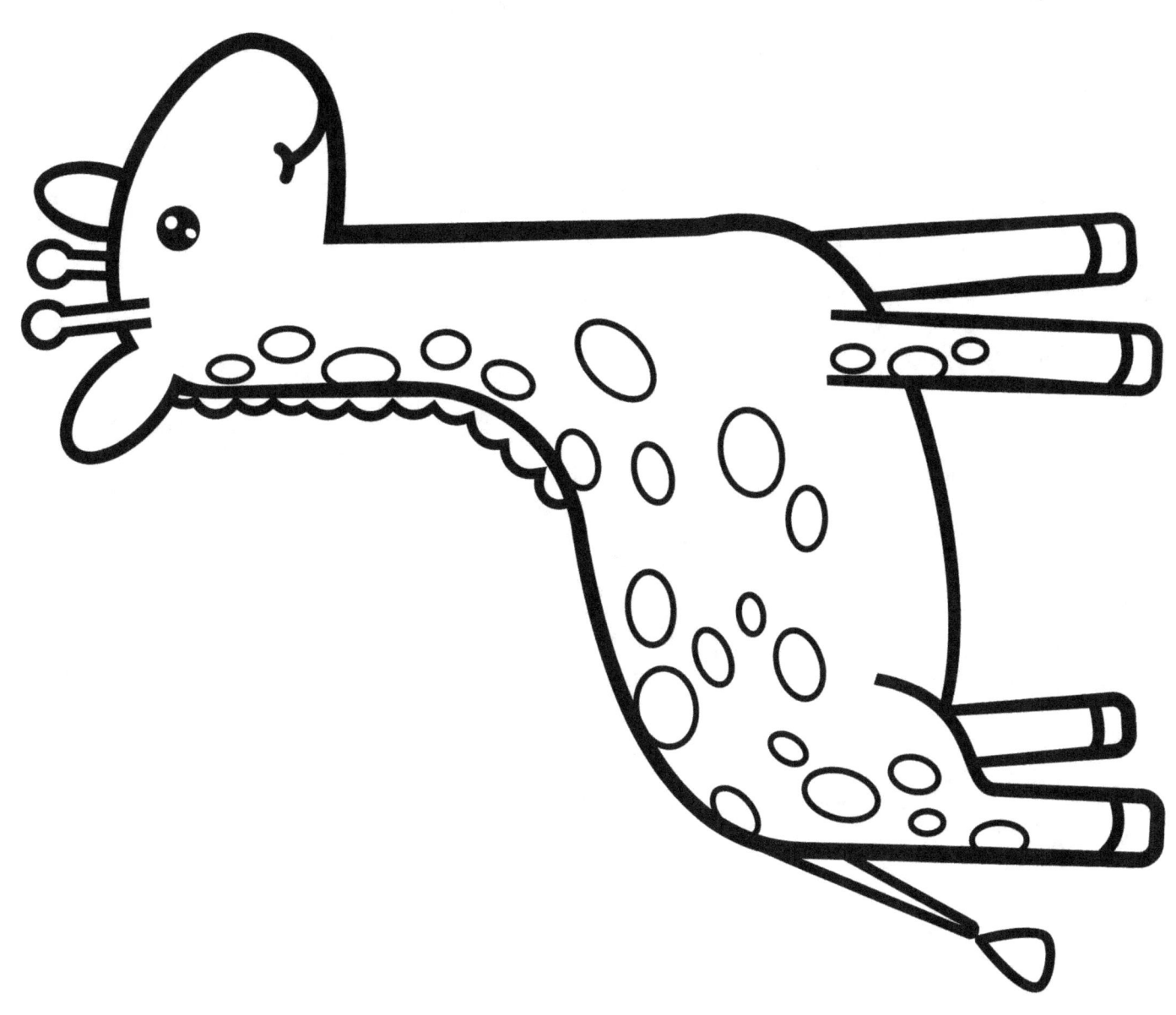

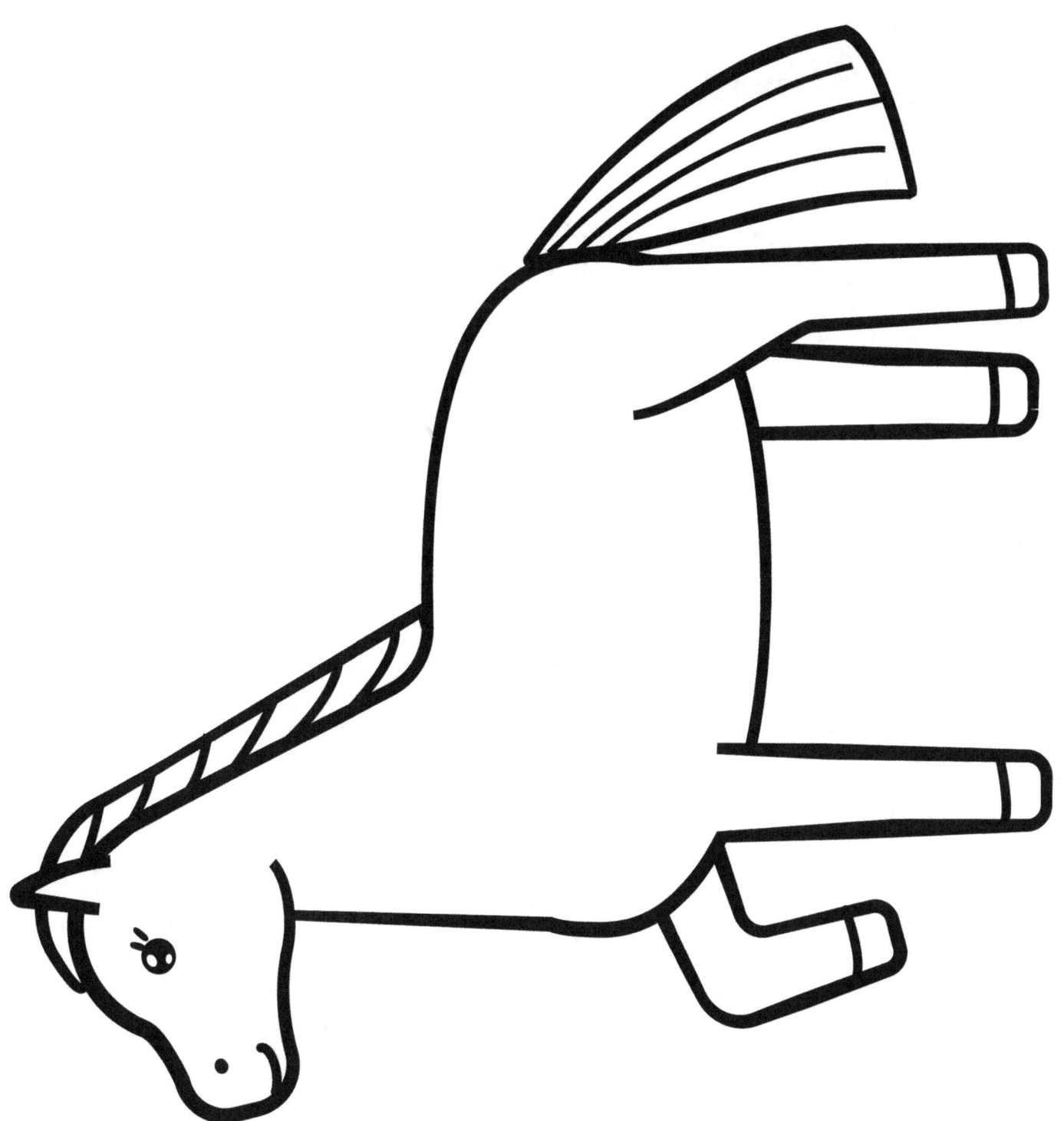

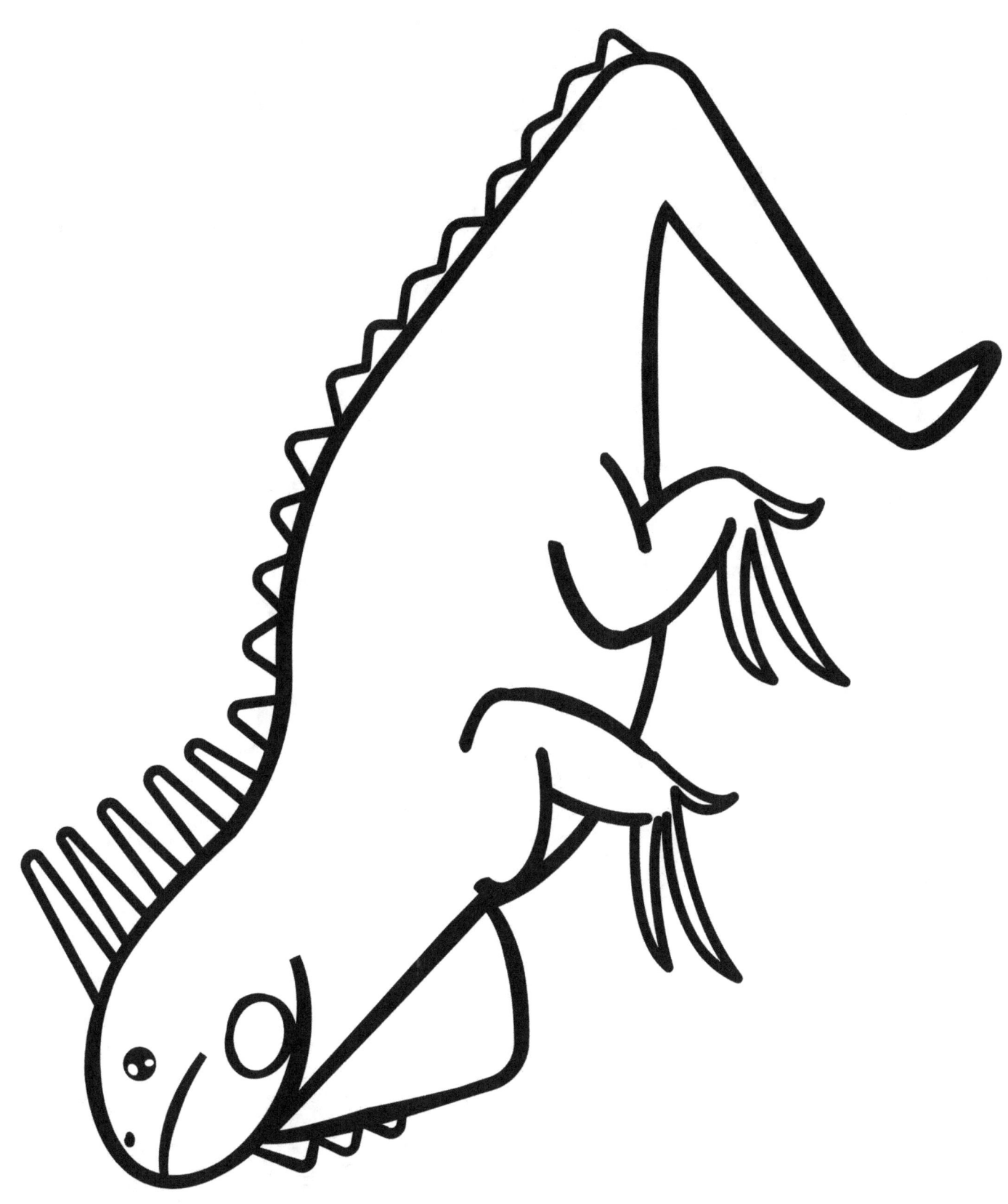

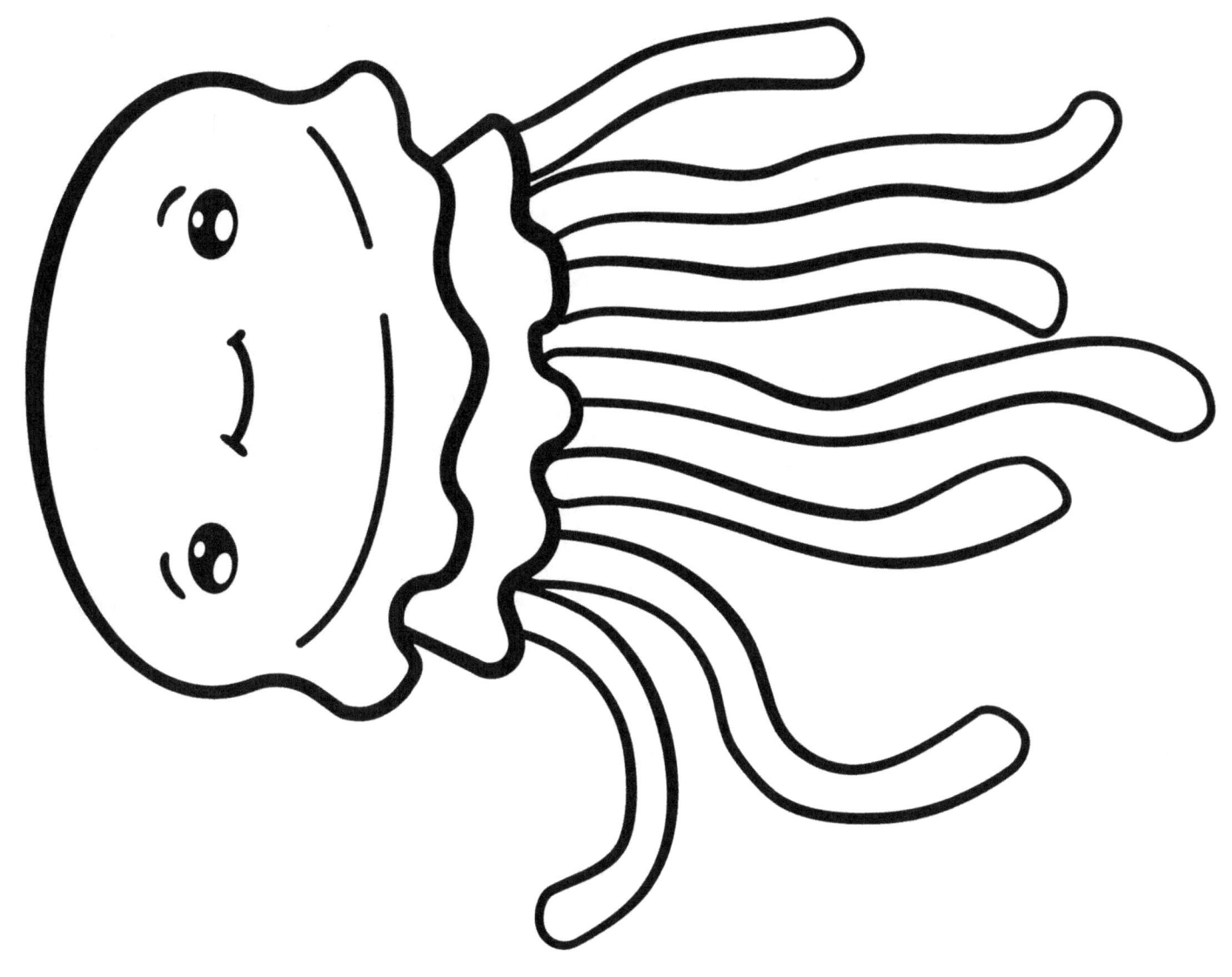

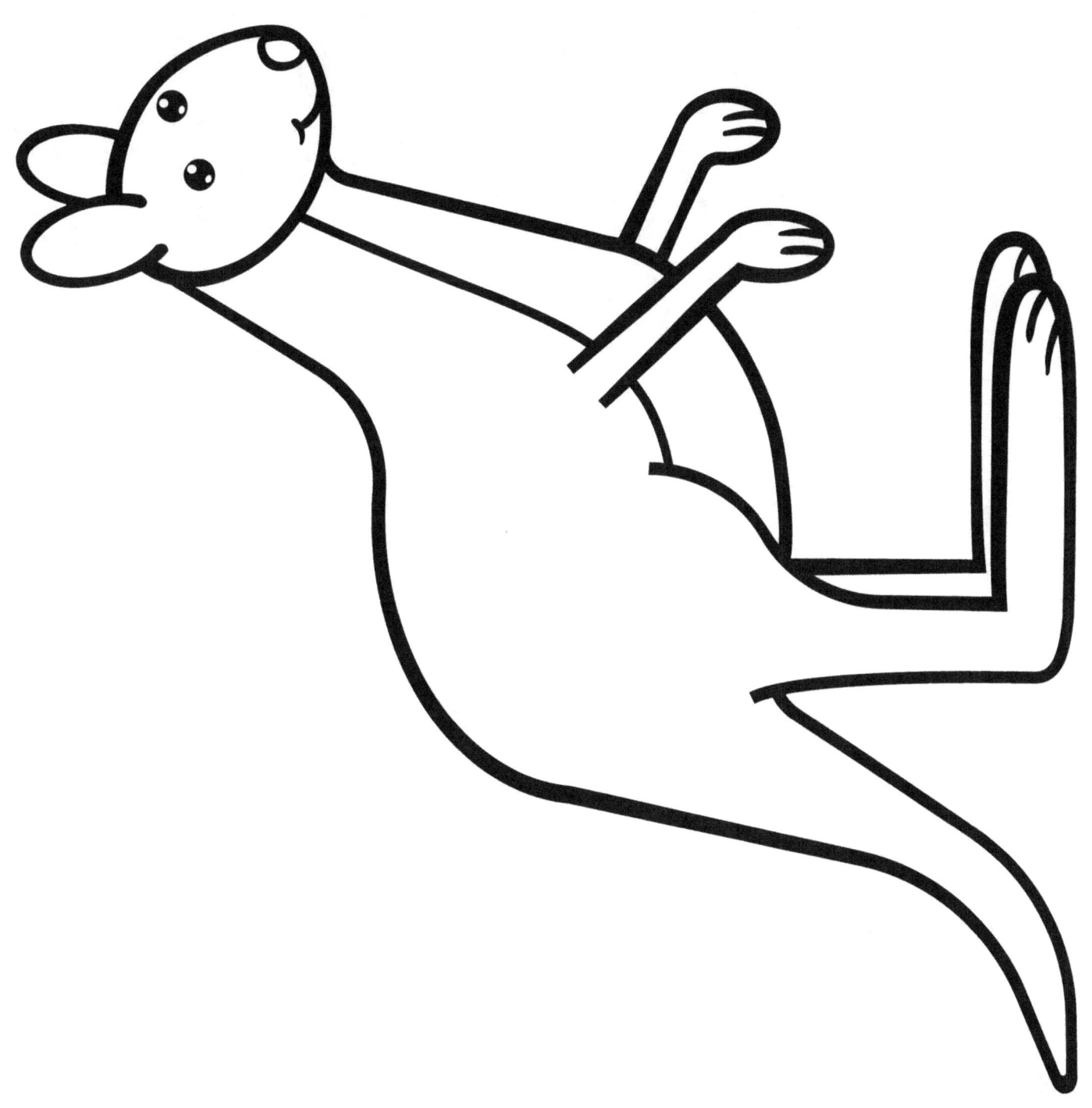

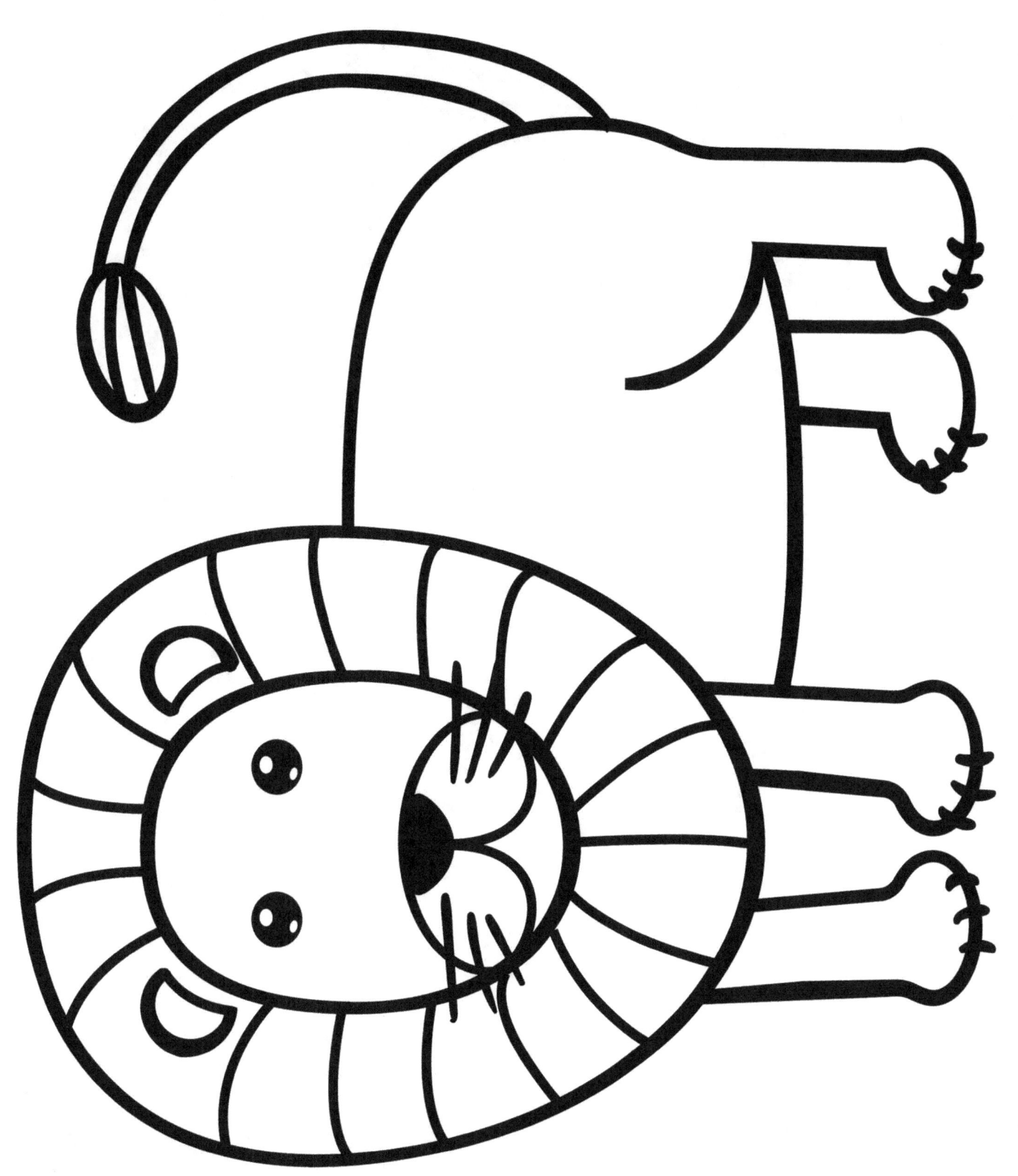

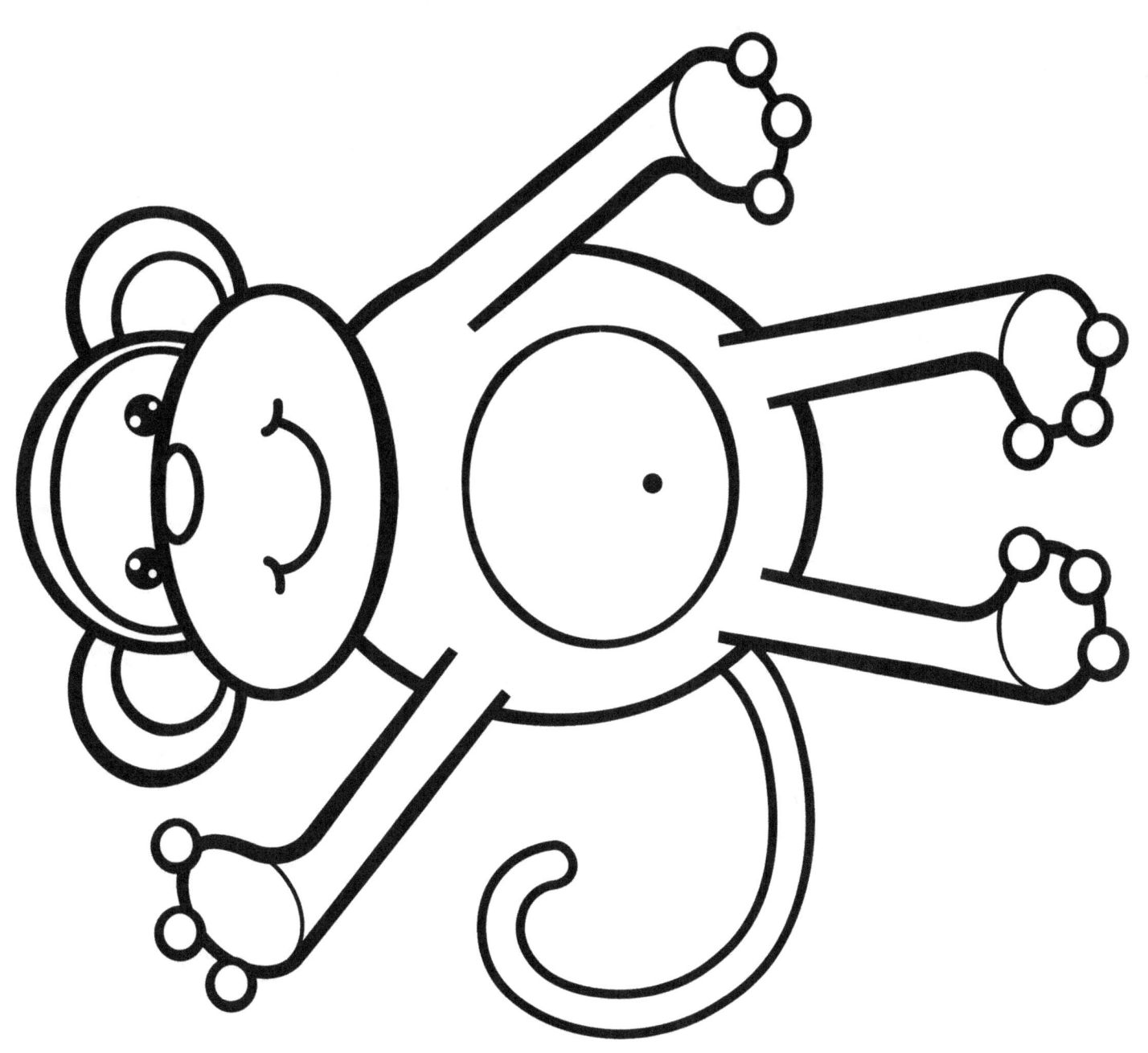

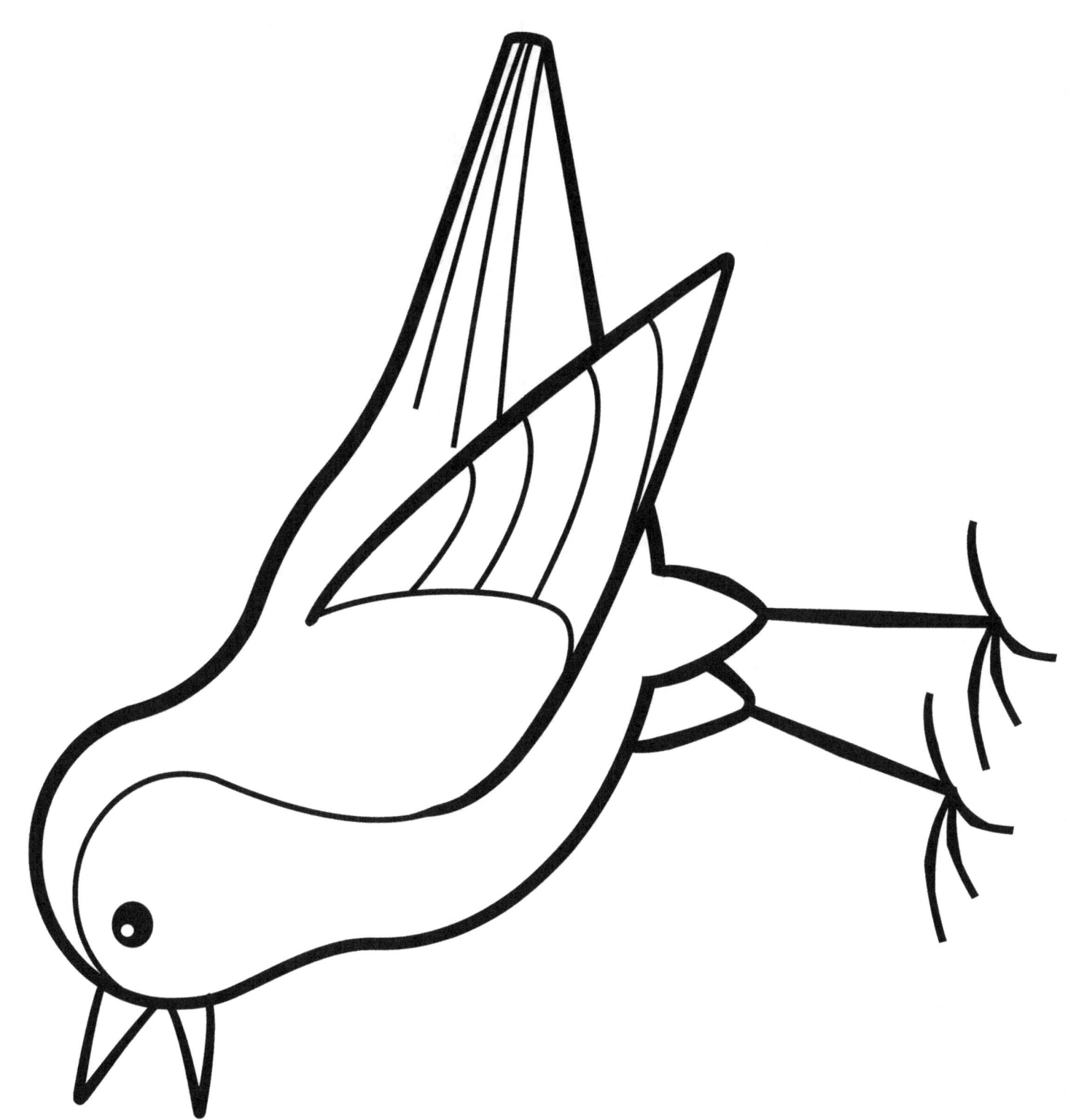

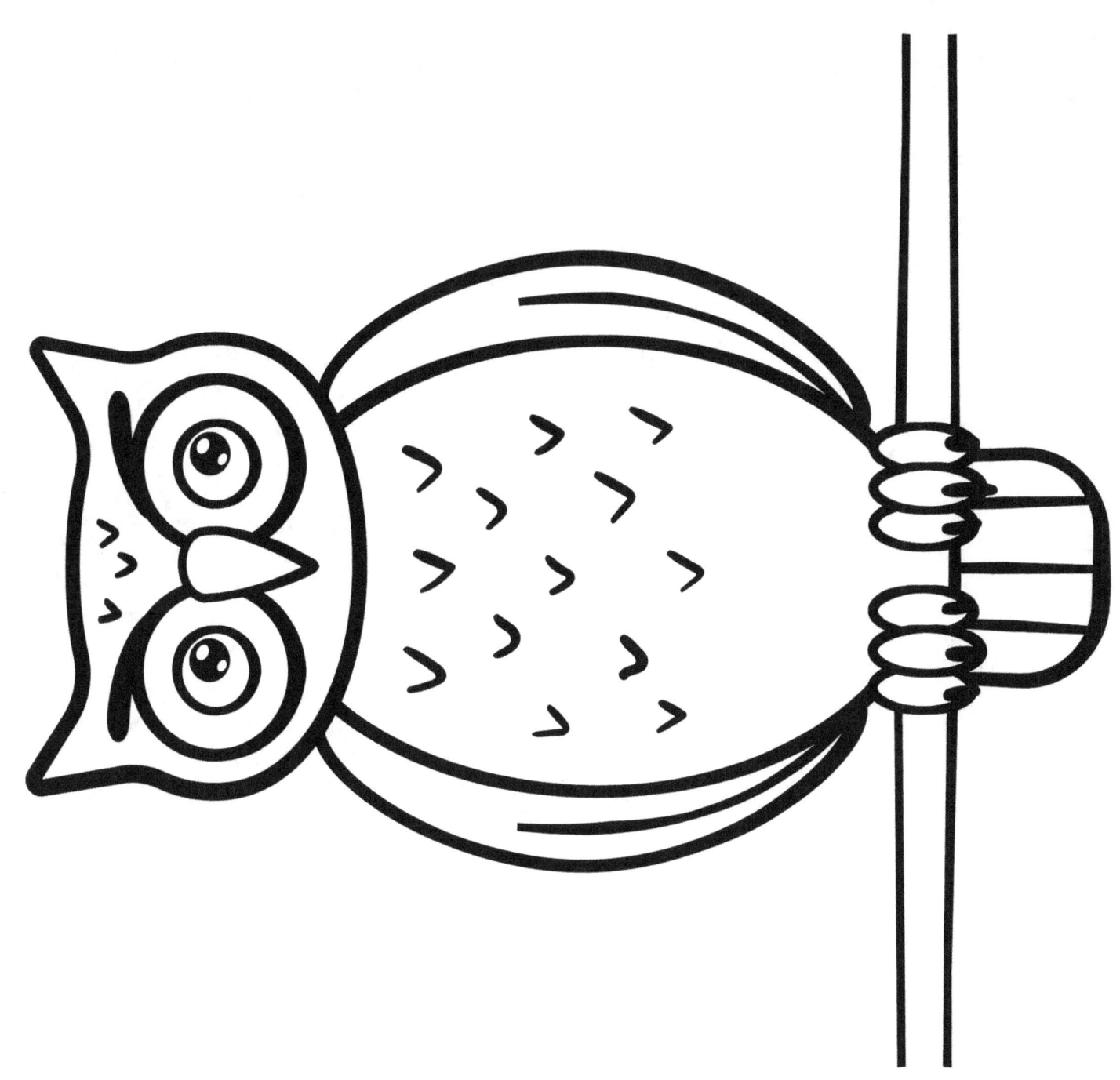

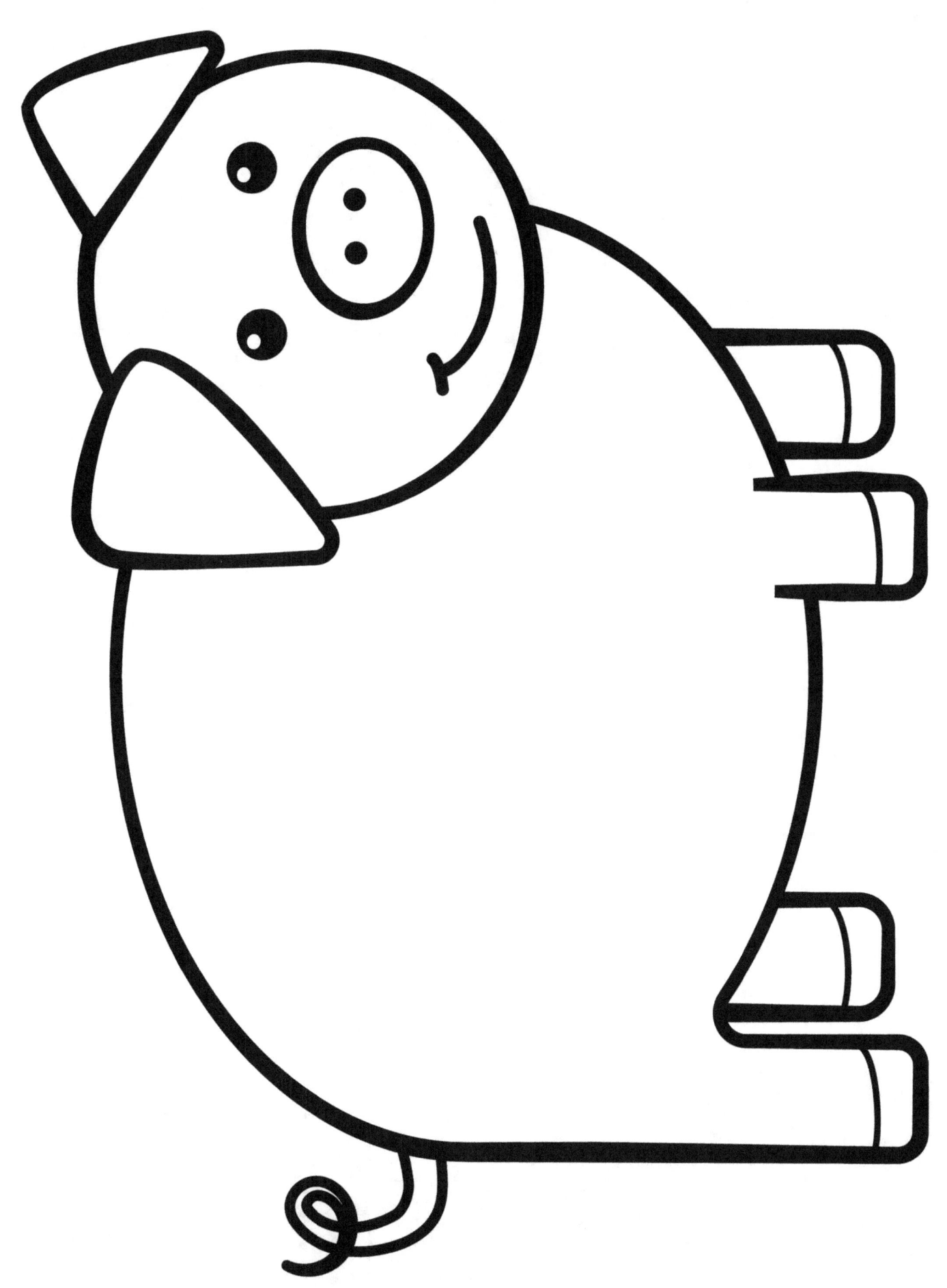

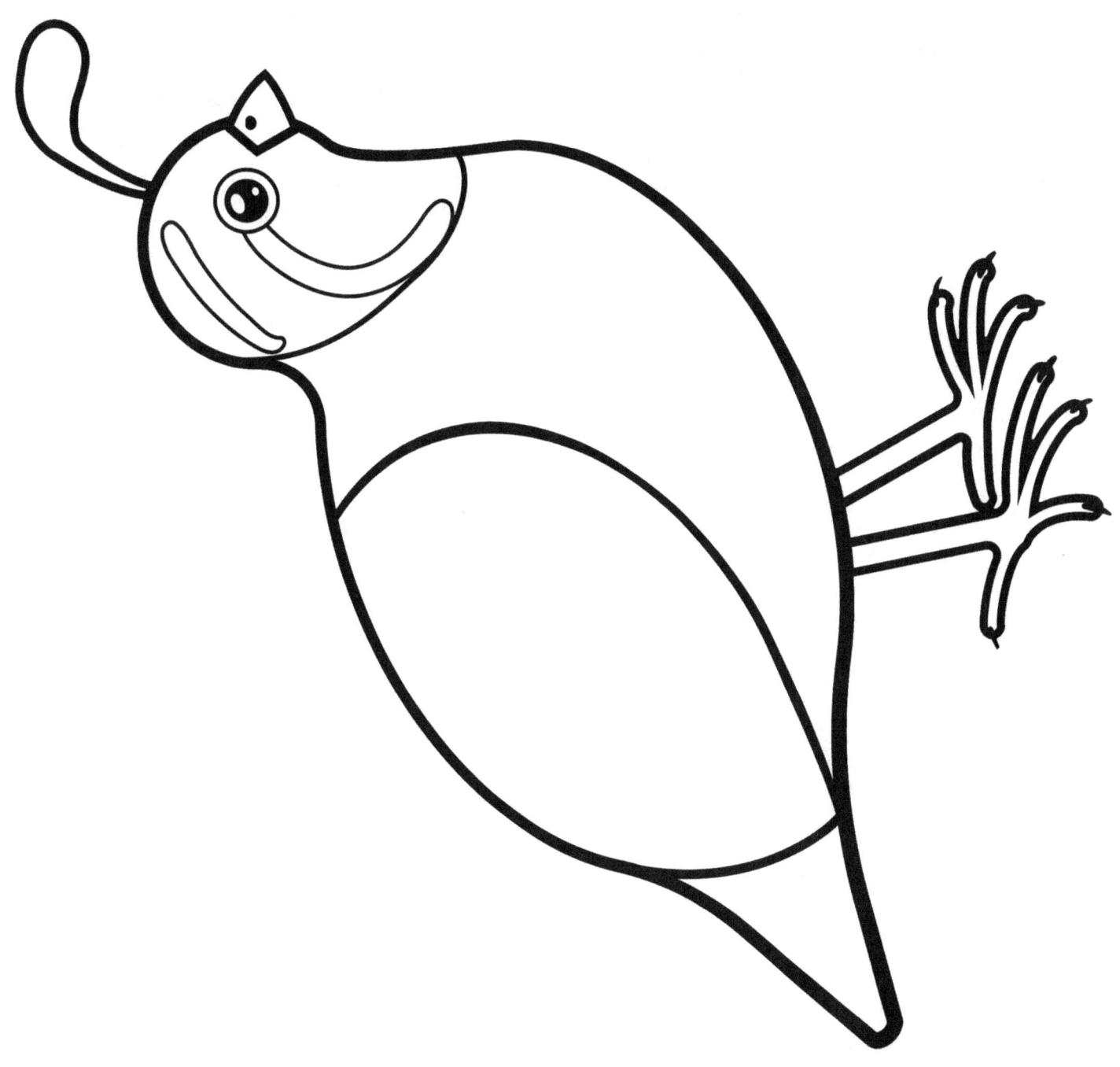

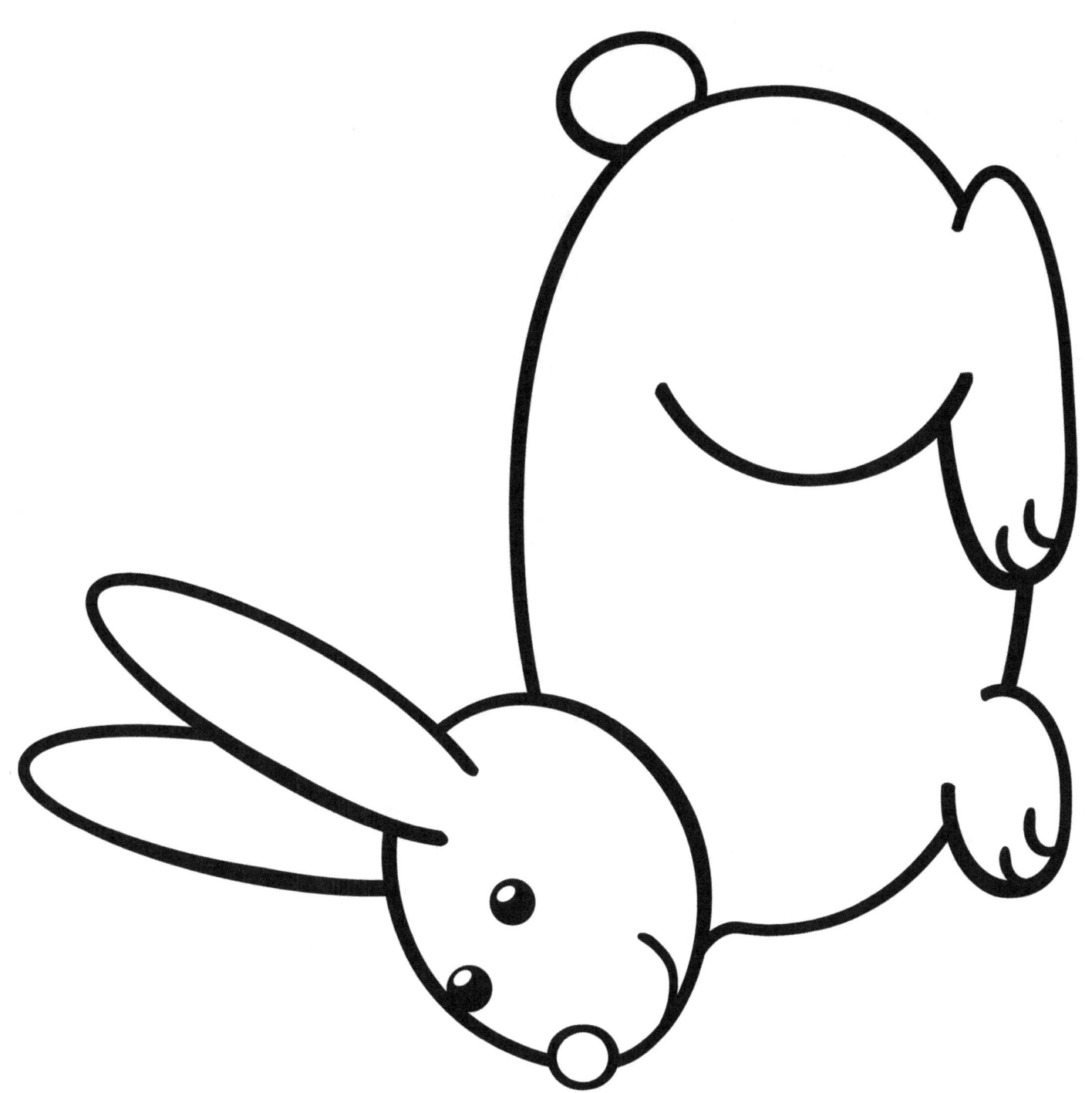

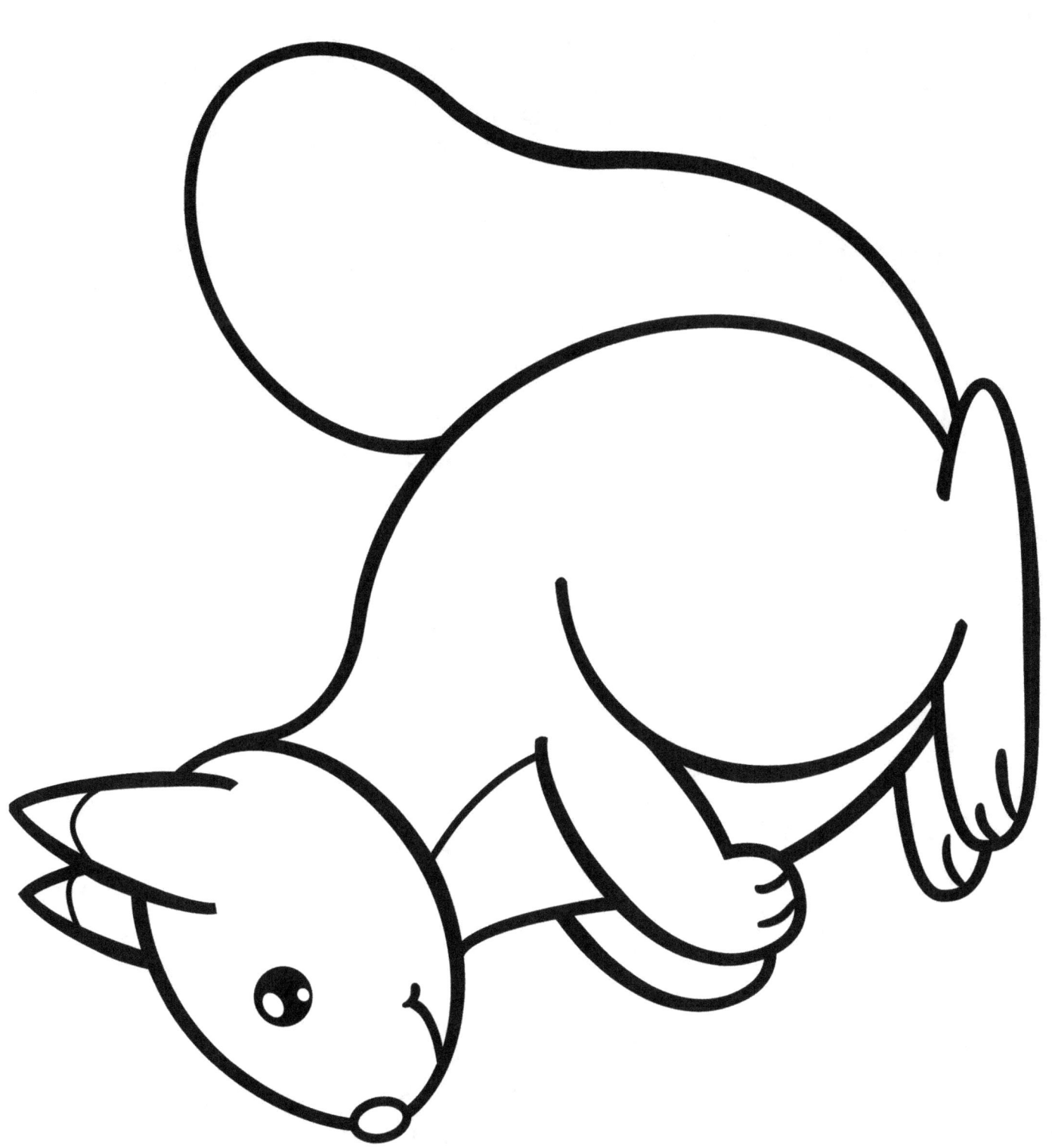

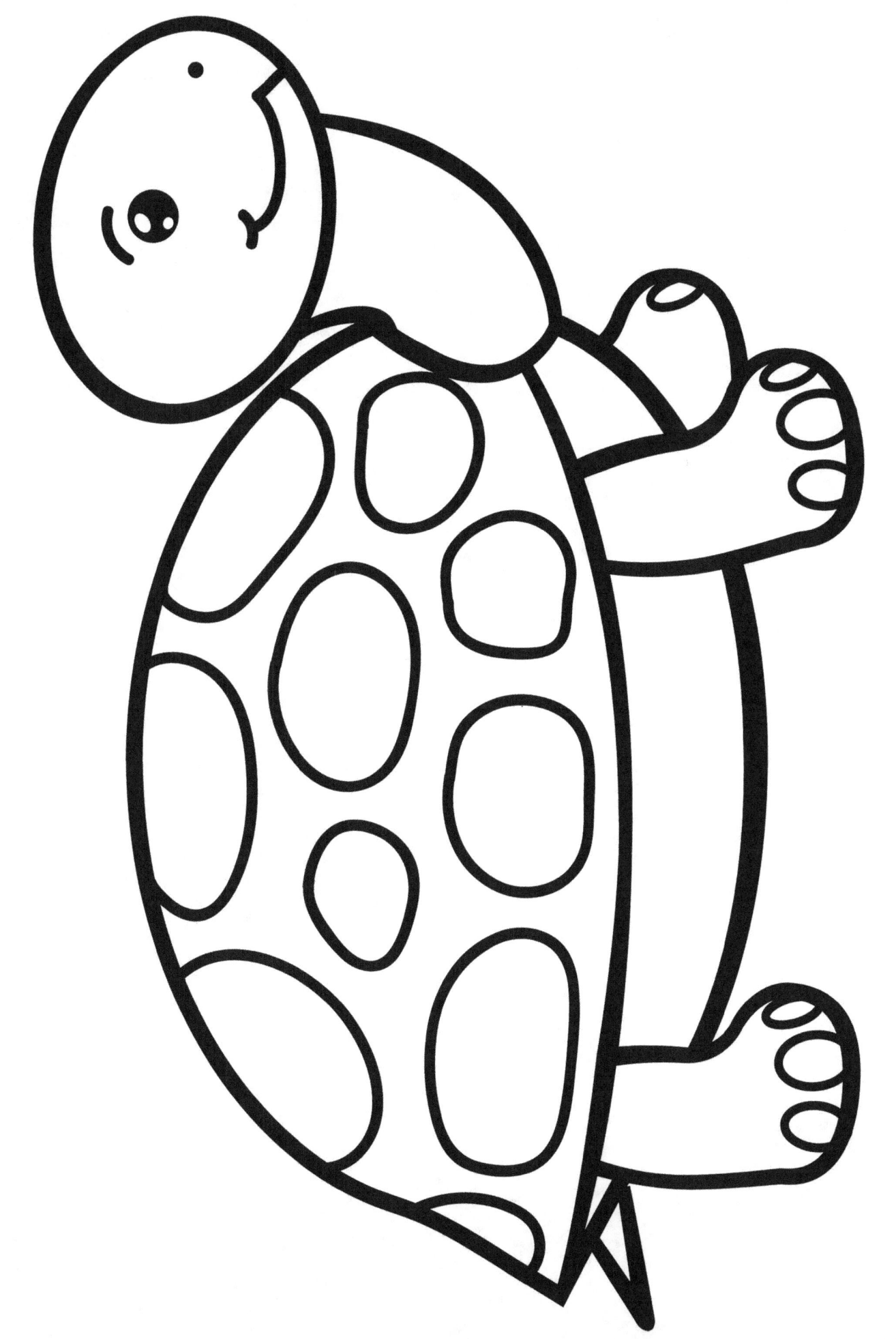

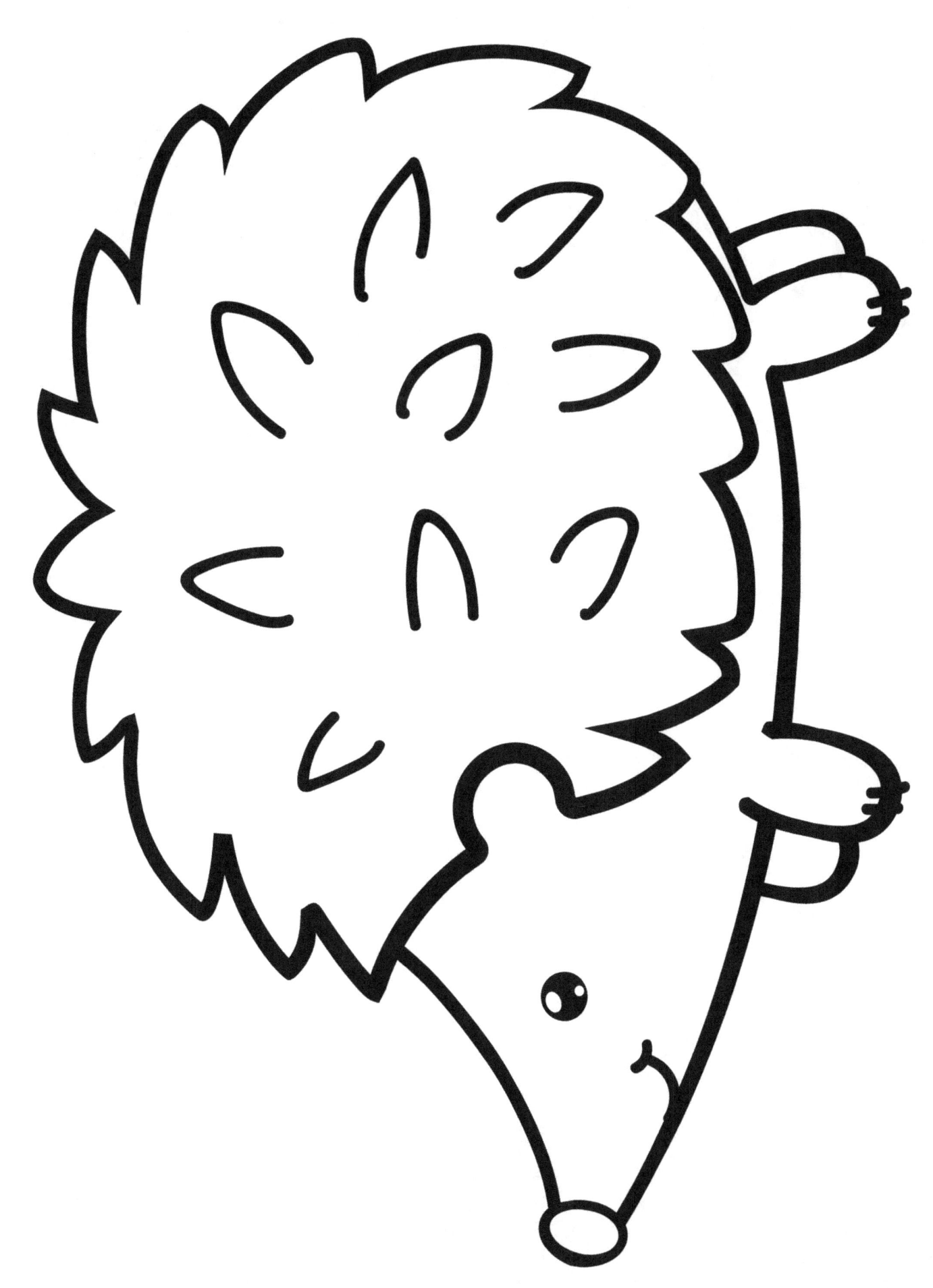

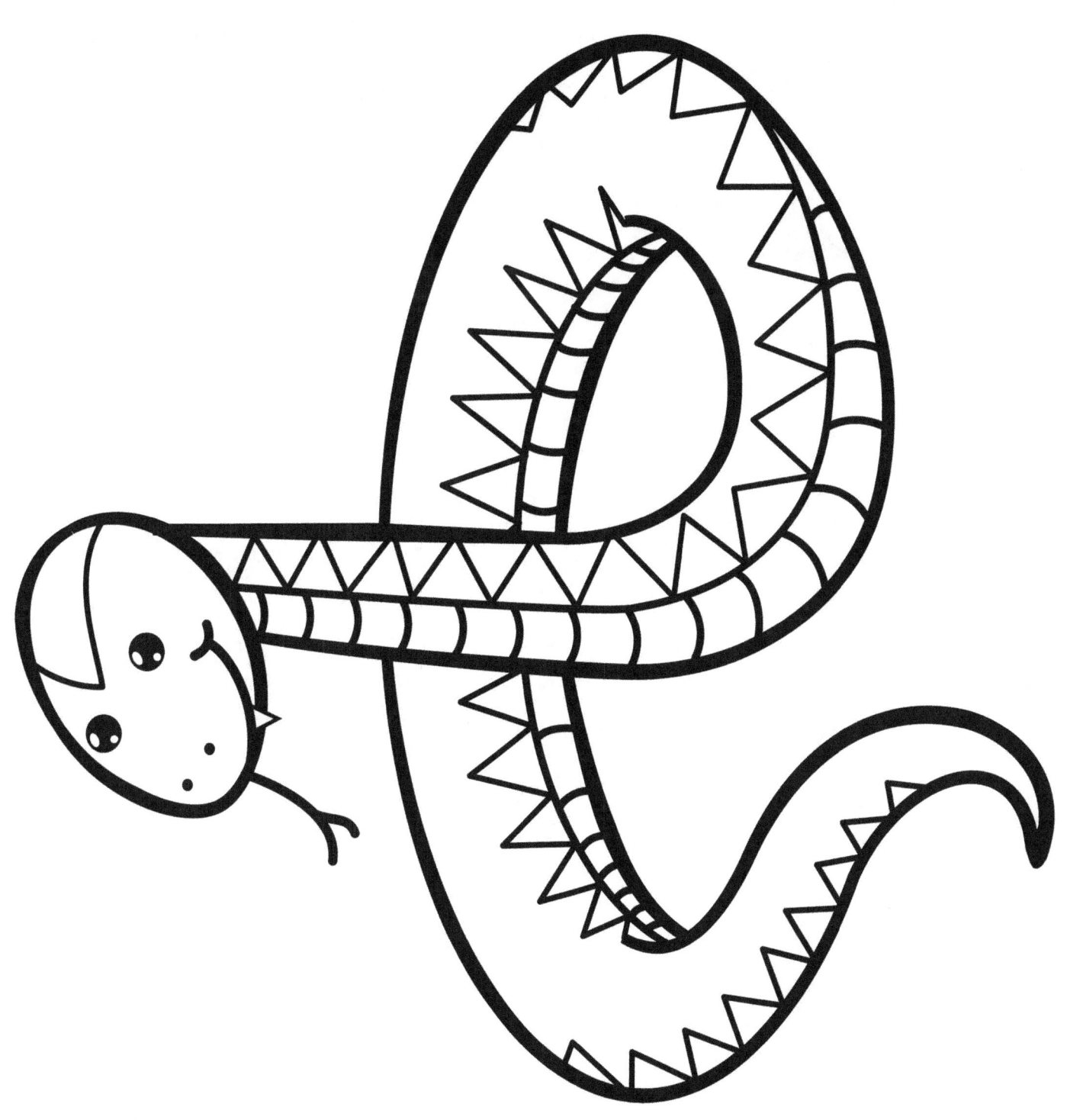

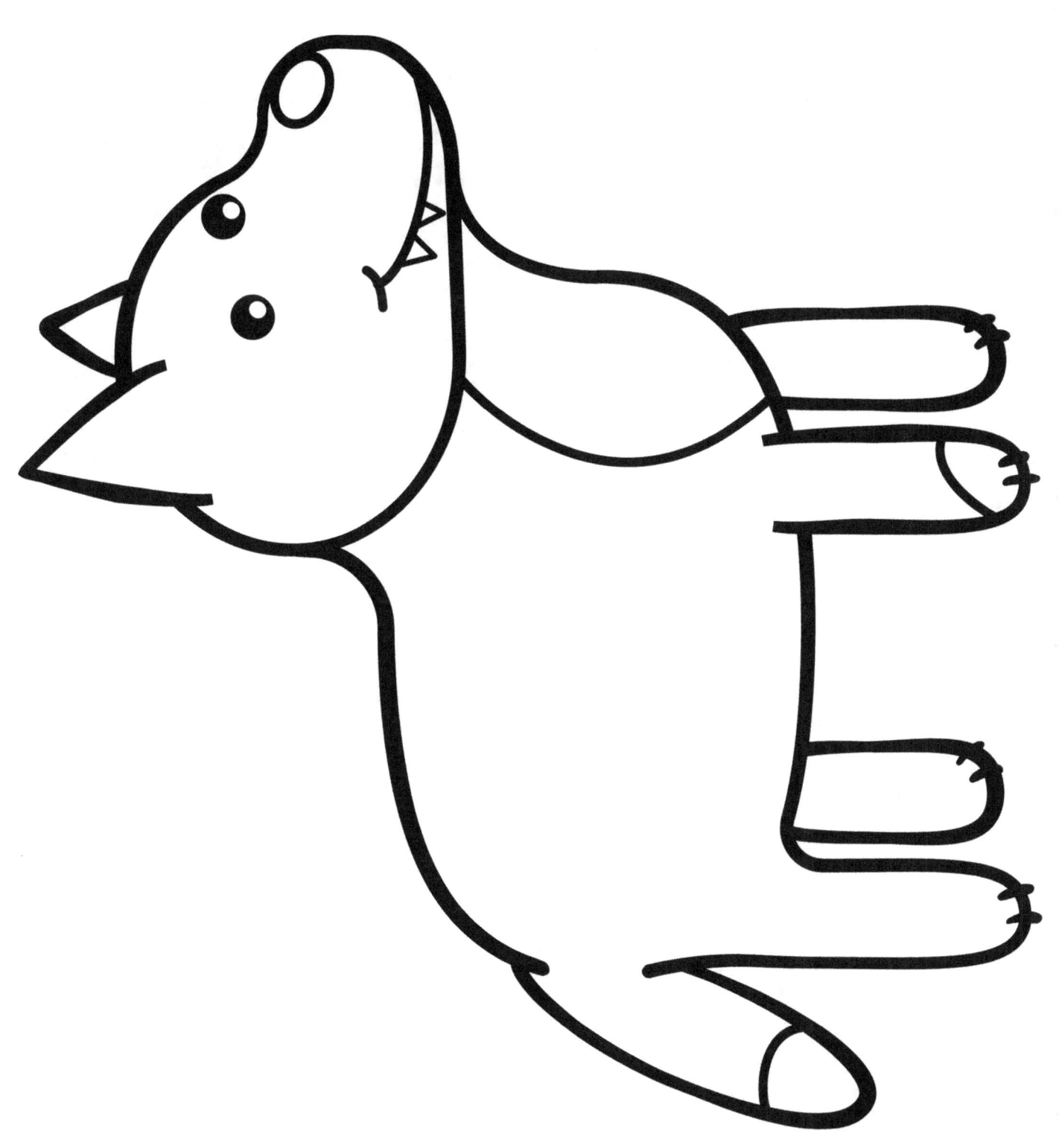

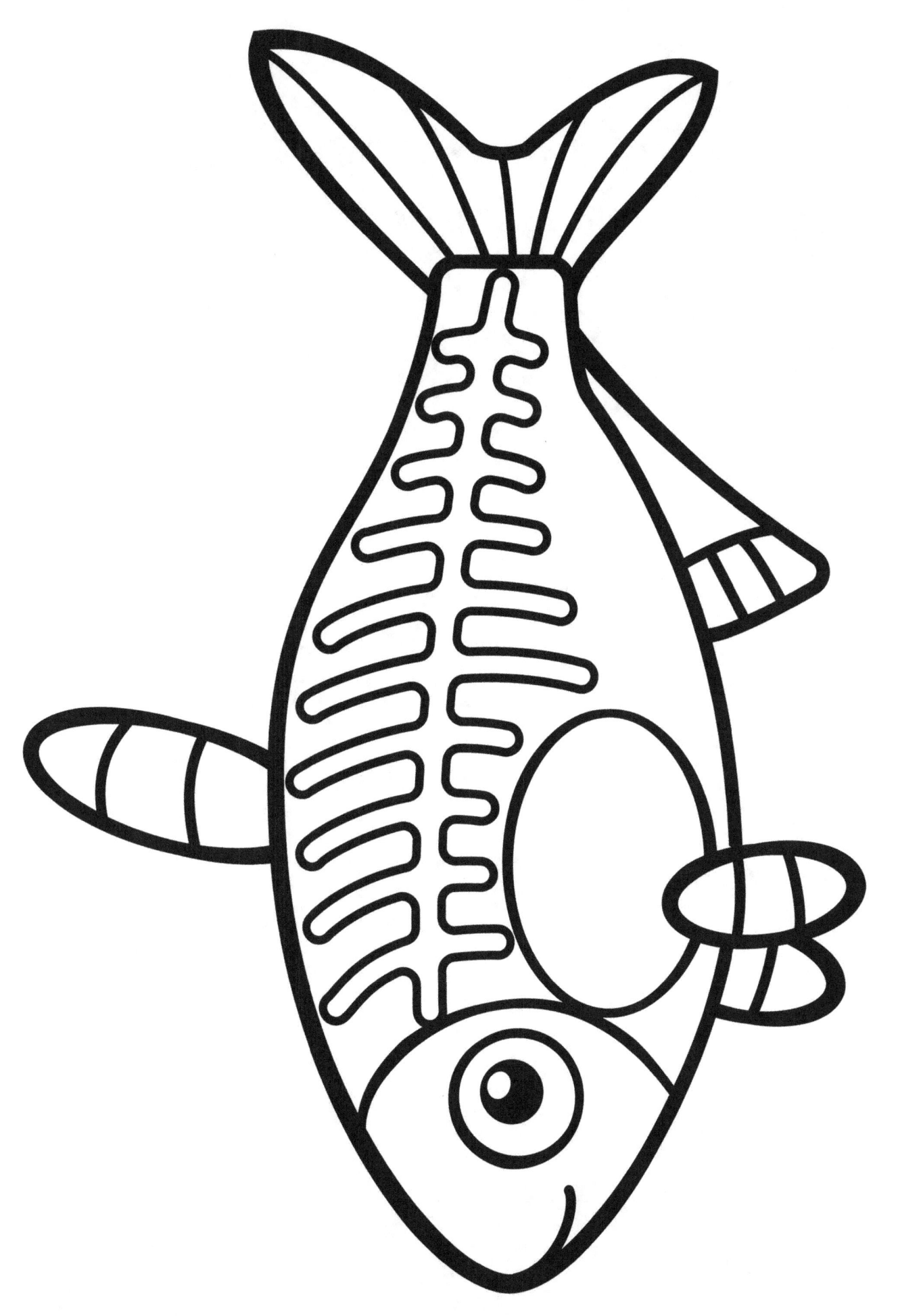

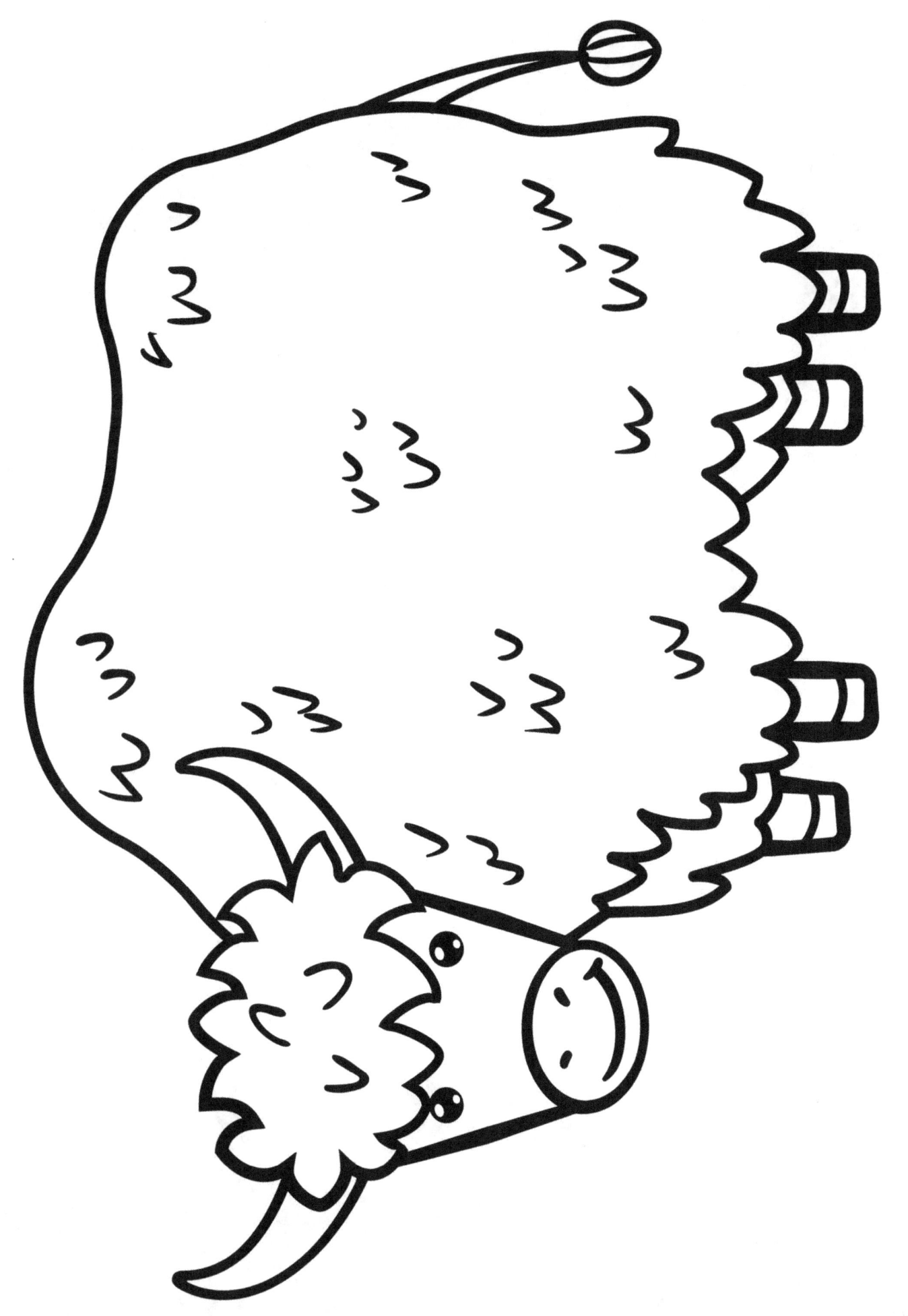

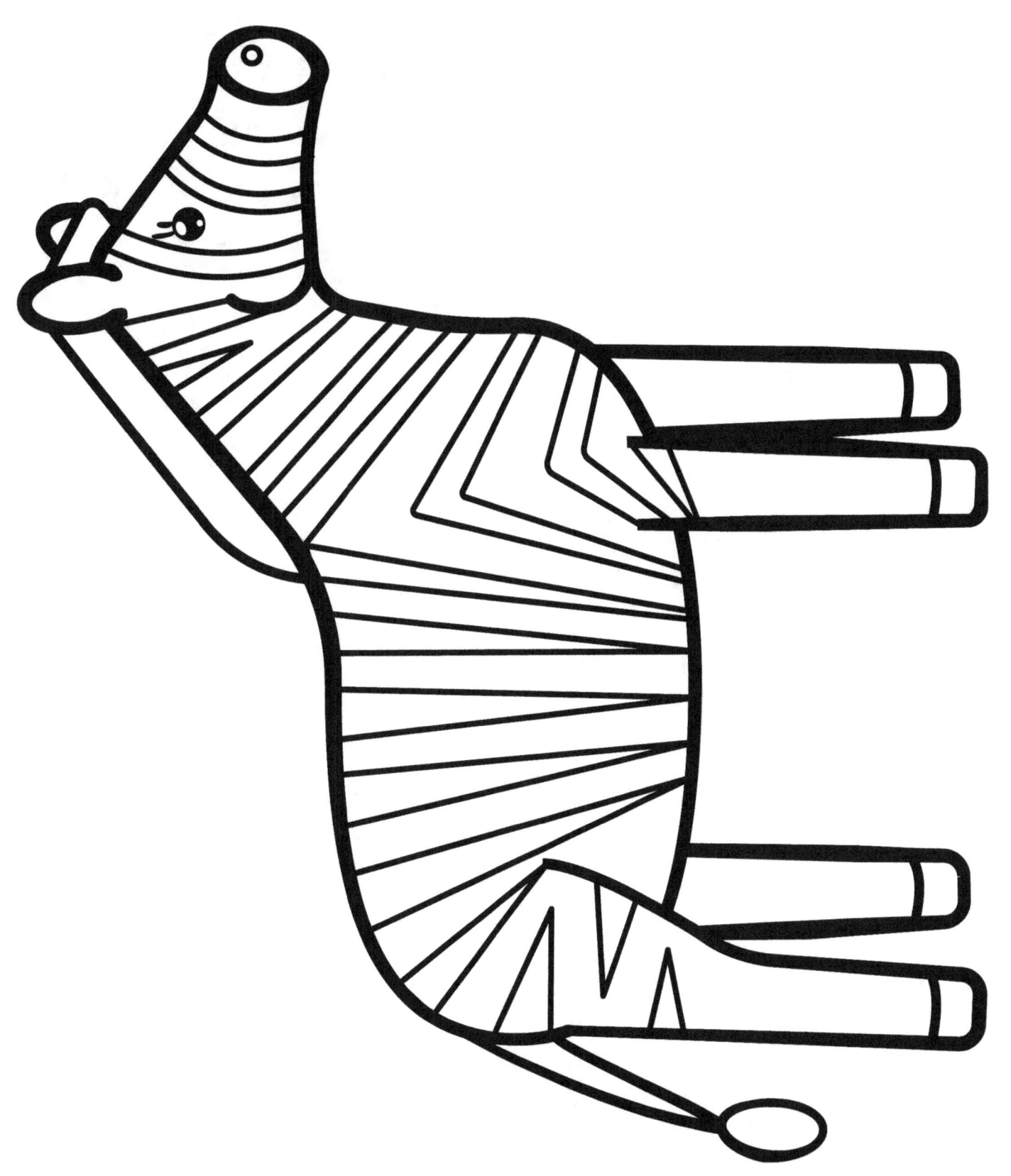

FREE PAGES FROM OUR BOOKS

THANK YOU for choosing our book, we hope you **LIKED IT**. Fill free to write **YOUR REVIEW** and show **YOUR ART-WORK** on **AMAZON**. We want to know **YOUR IM-PRESSION** of the book.

And we want to **PRESENT YOU** pages from our other books:

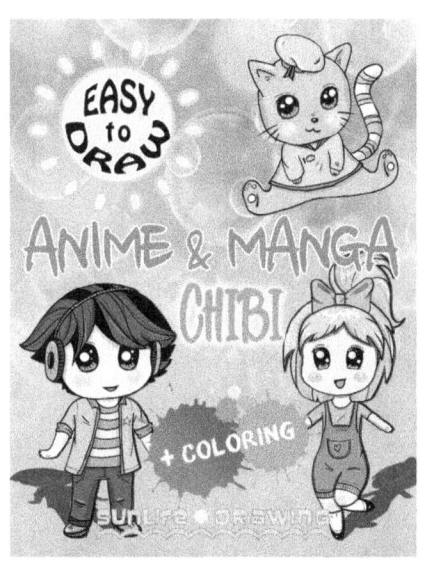
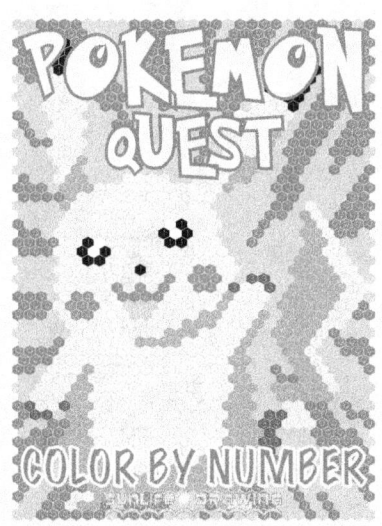
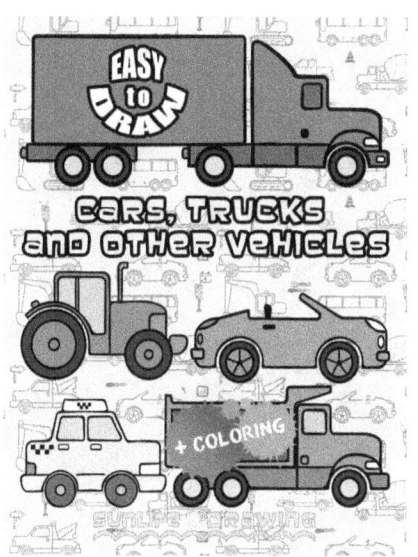

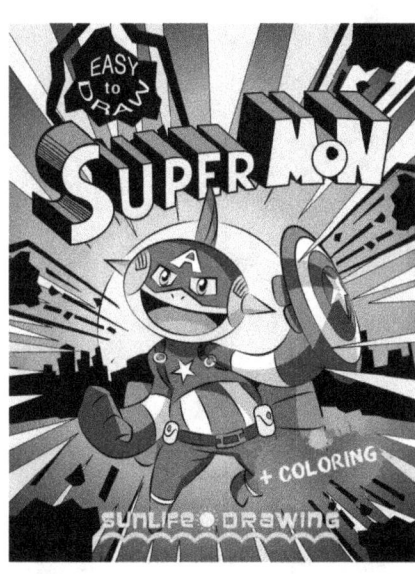
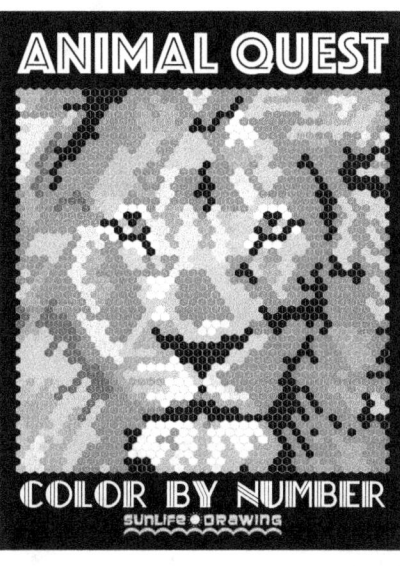
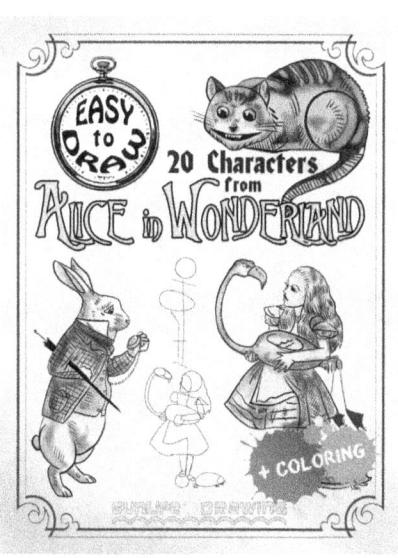

CHIBI JOYFUL GIRL

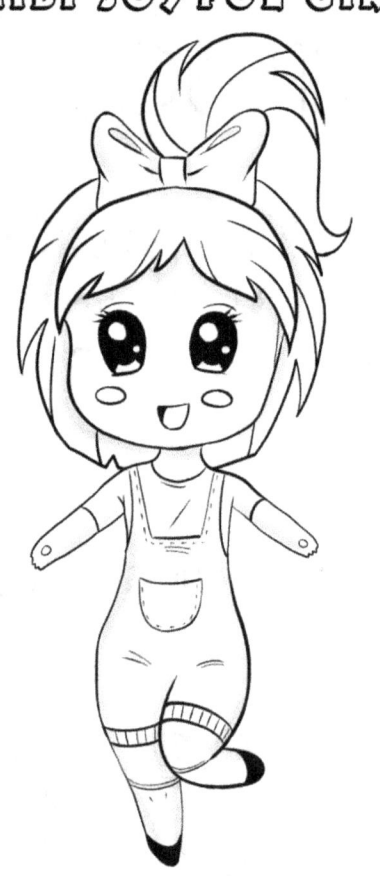

1.

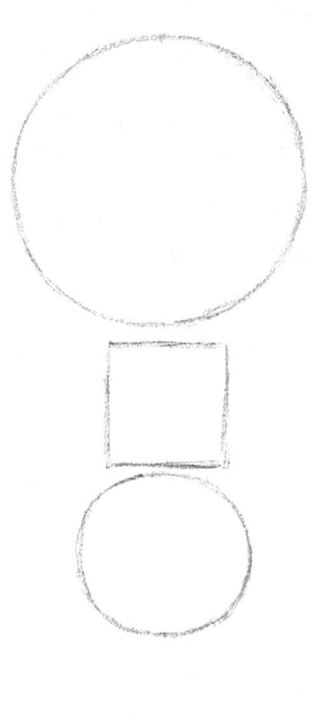

2.

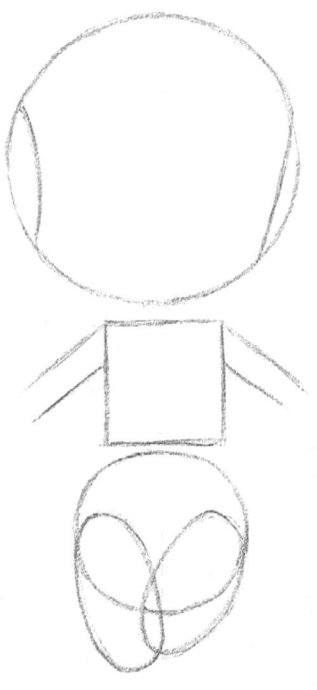

3.

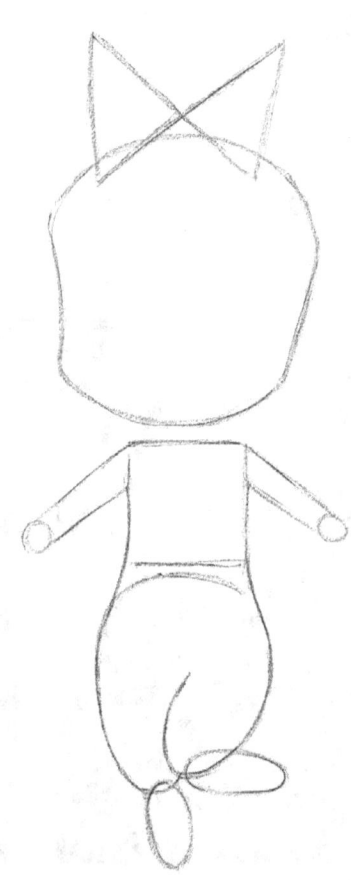

4.

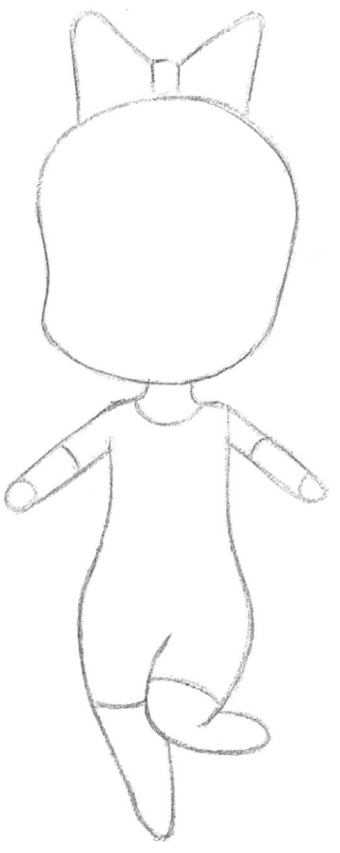

5.

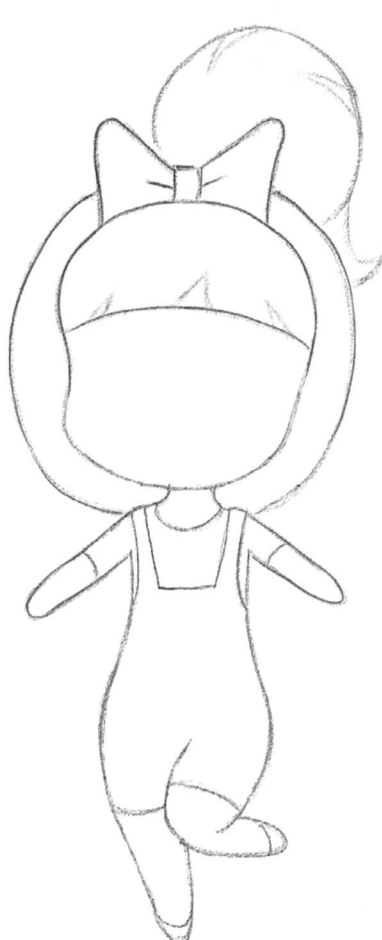

6.

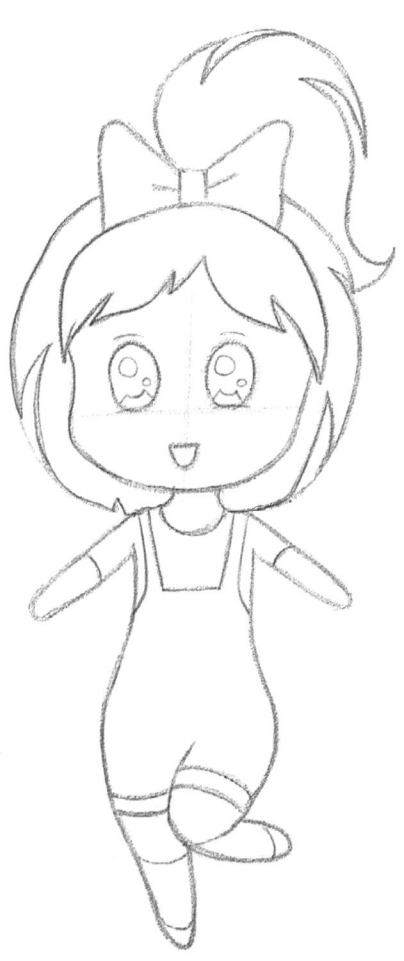

7.

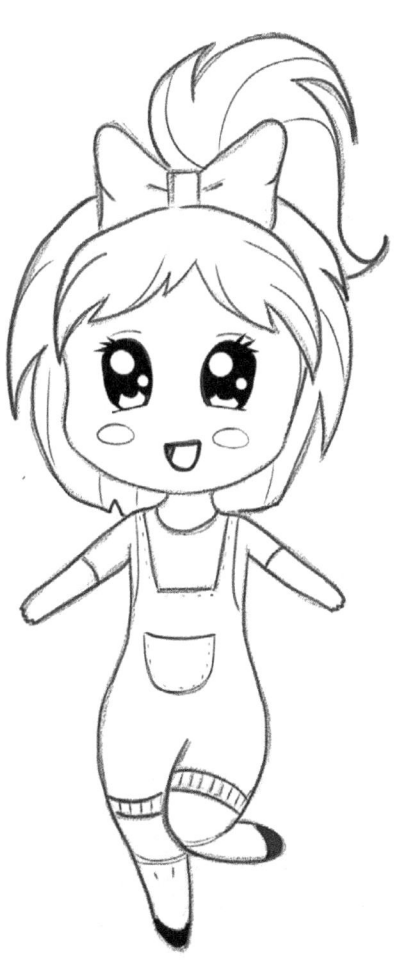

1	BLACK	
2	GRAY	
3	BROWN	
4	RED	
5	ORANGE	
6	YELLOW	
7	BRIGHT GREEN	
8	GREEN	
9	BLUE	
10	SKY BLUE	
11	PURPLE	
12	PINK	

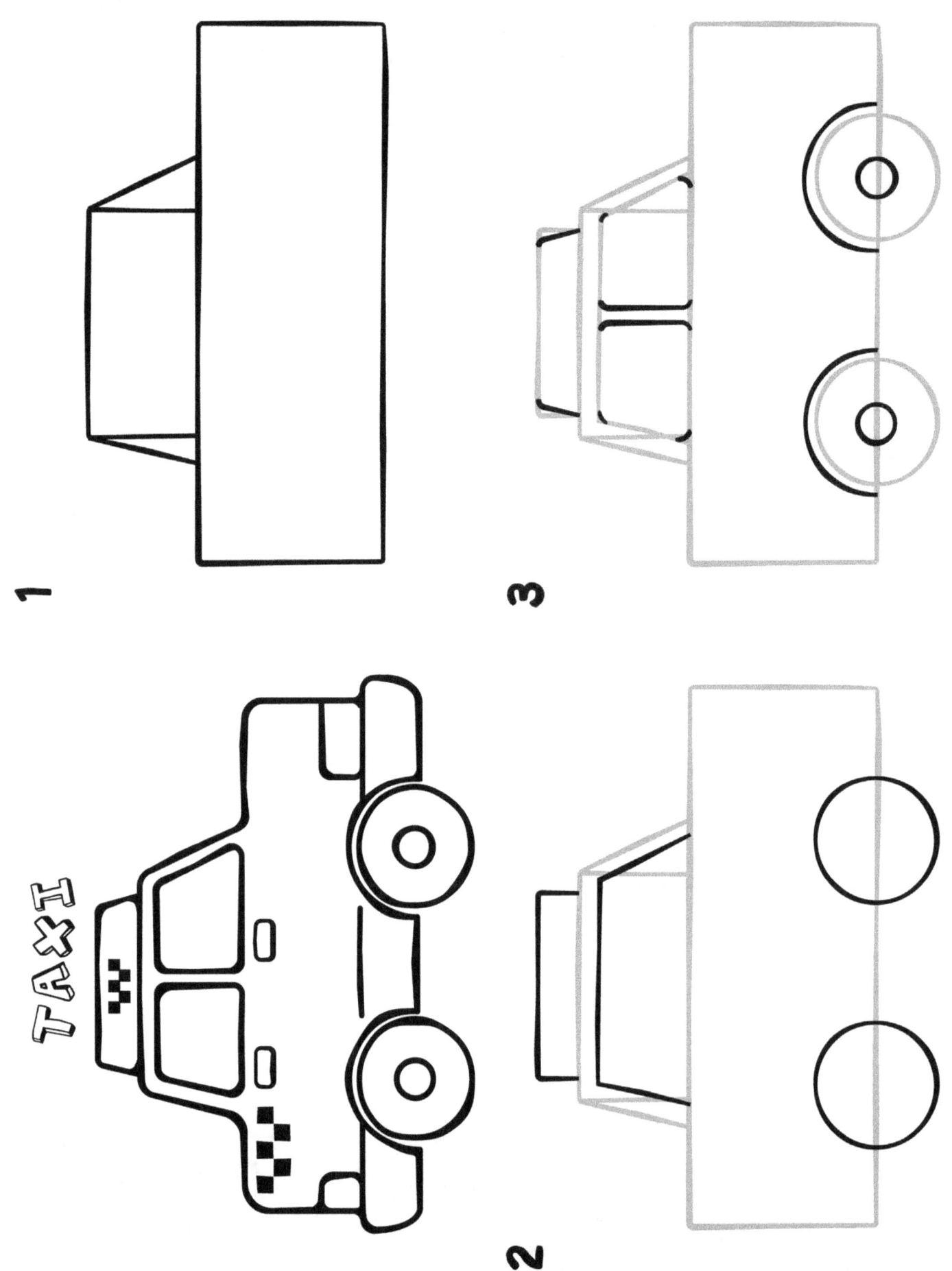

5

4

6

CaptainShtomp 1.

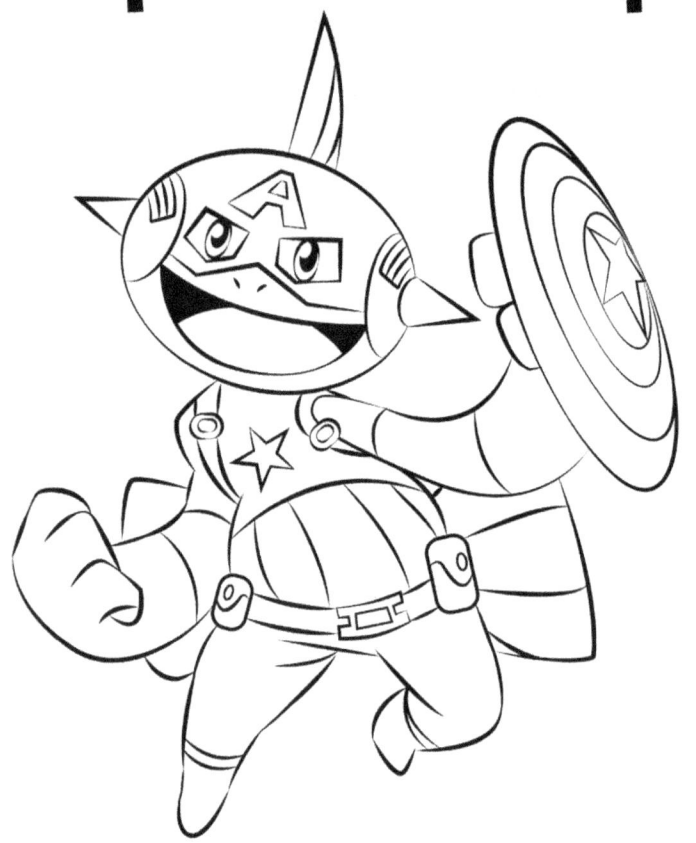
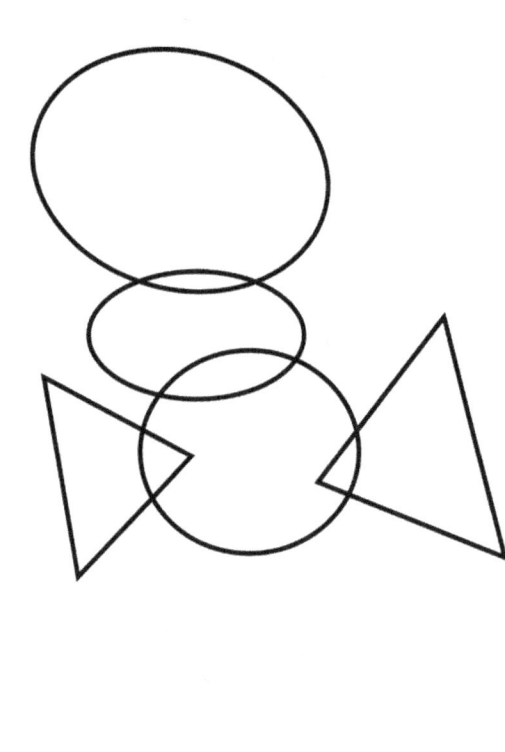

2.

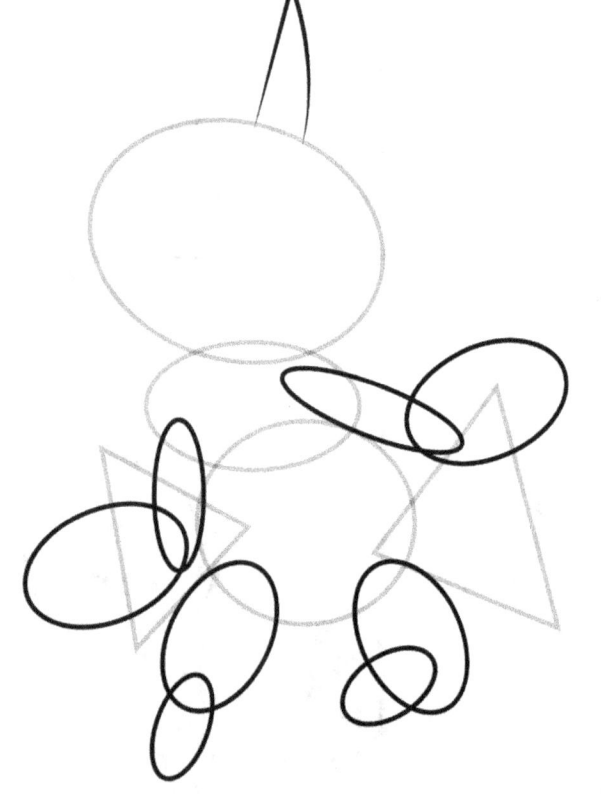

3.

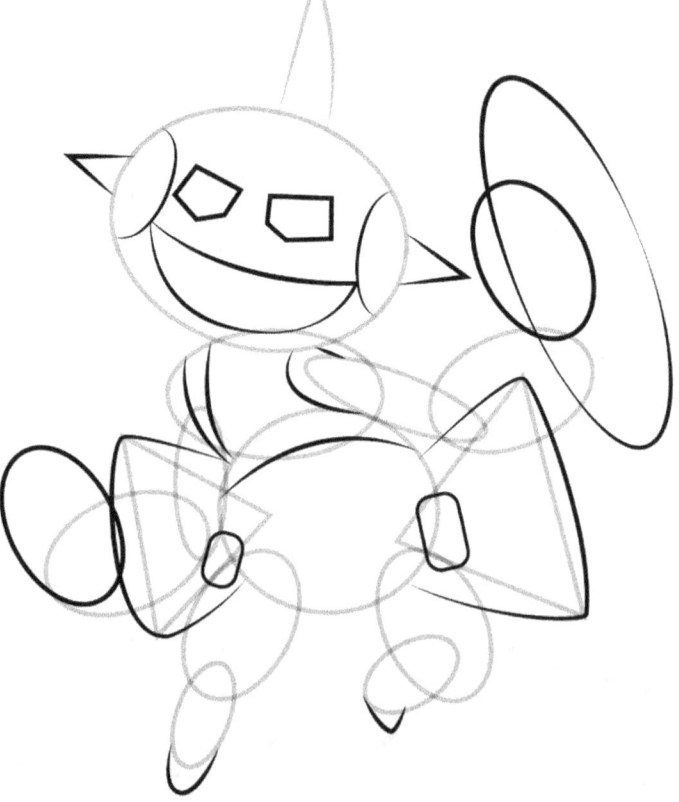

4.

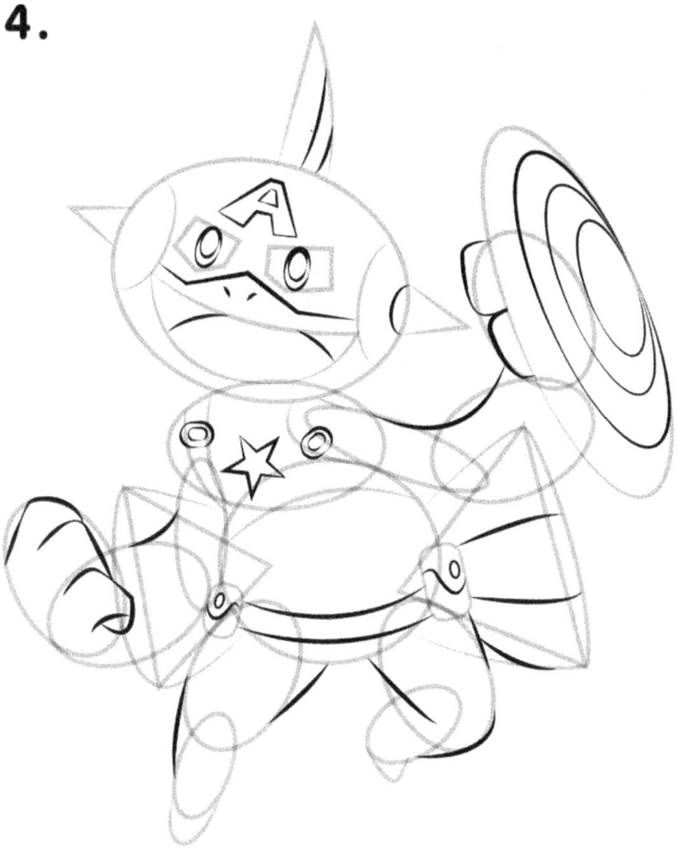

5.

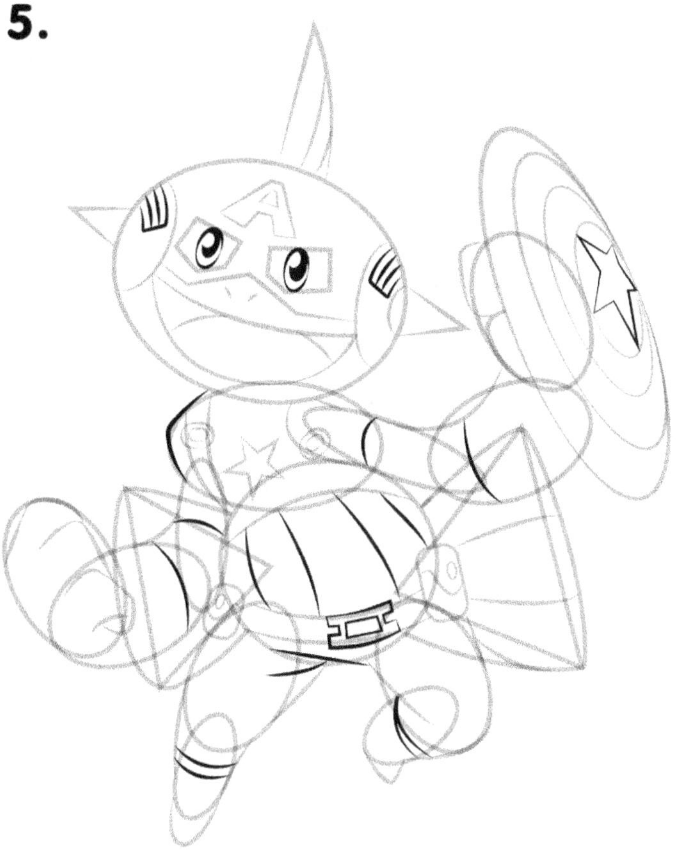

6.

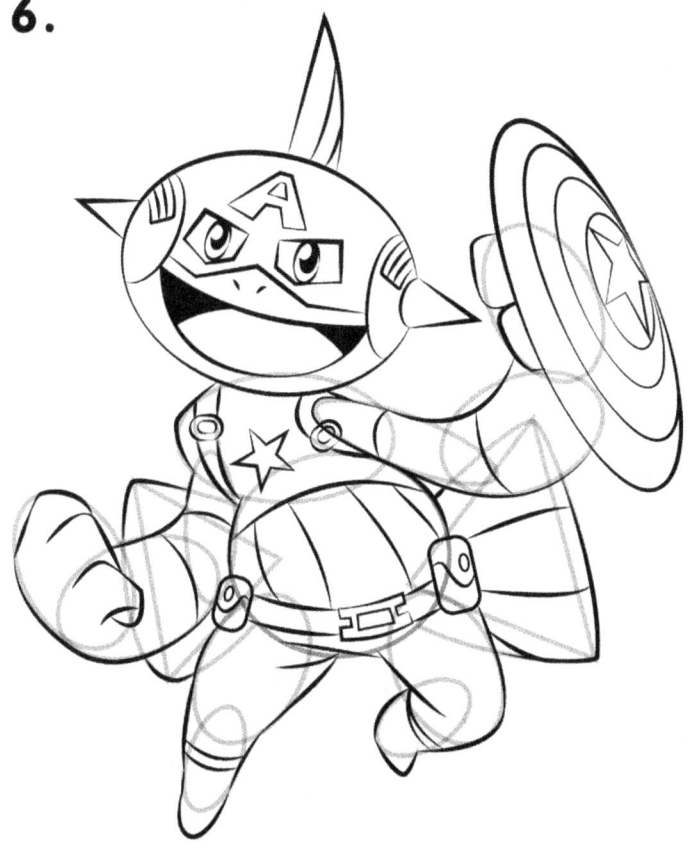

1	BLACK	
2	GRAY	
3	BROWN	
4	RED	
5	ORANGE	
6	YELLOW	
7	BRIGHT GREEN	
8	GREEN	
9	BLUE	
10	SKY BLUE	
11	PURPLE	
12	PINK	

ALICE WITH FLAMINGO

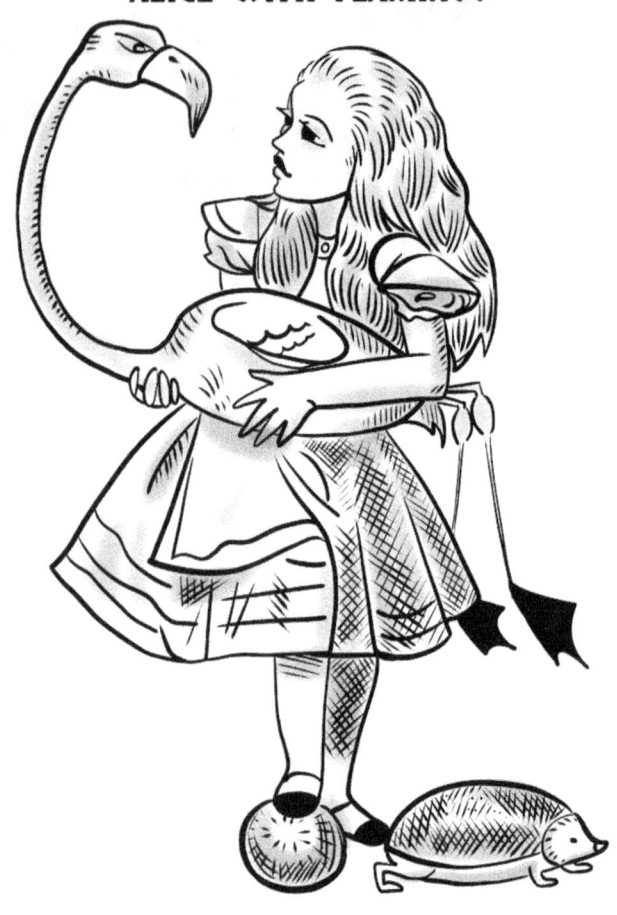

1.

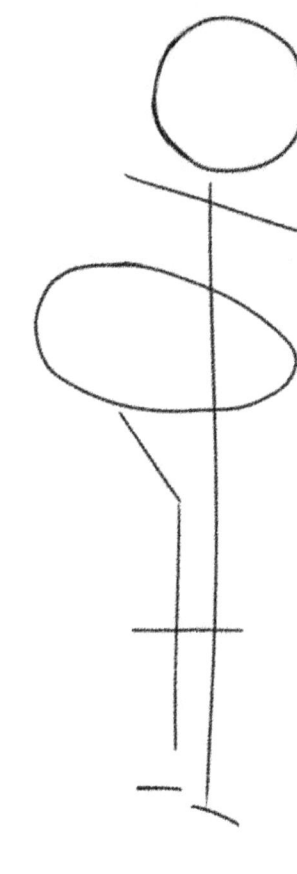

2.

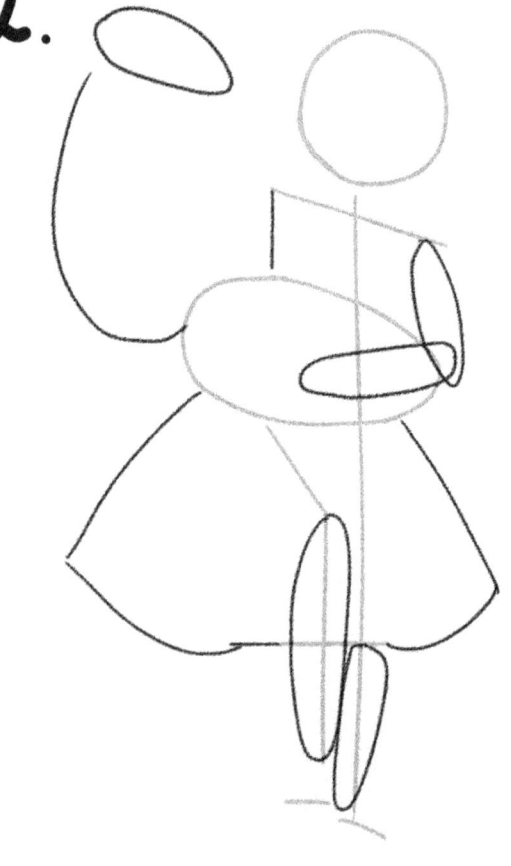

3.

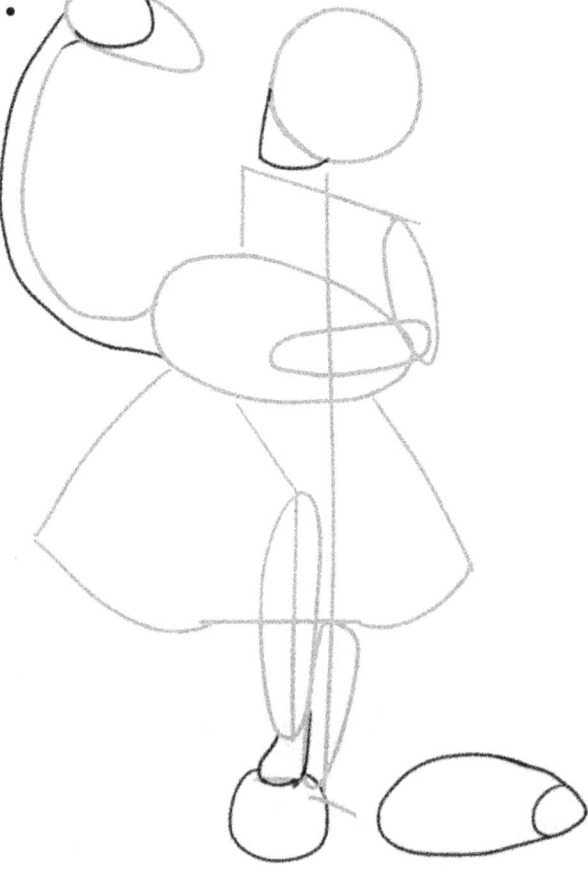

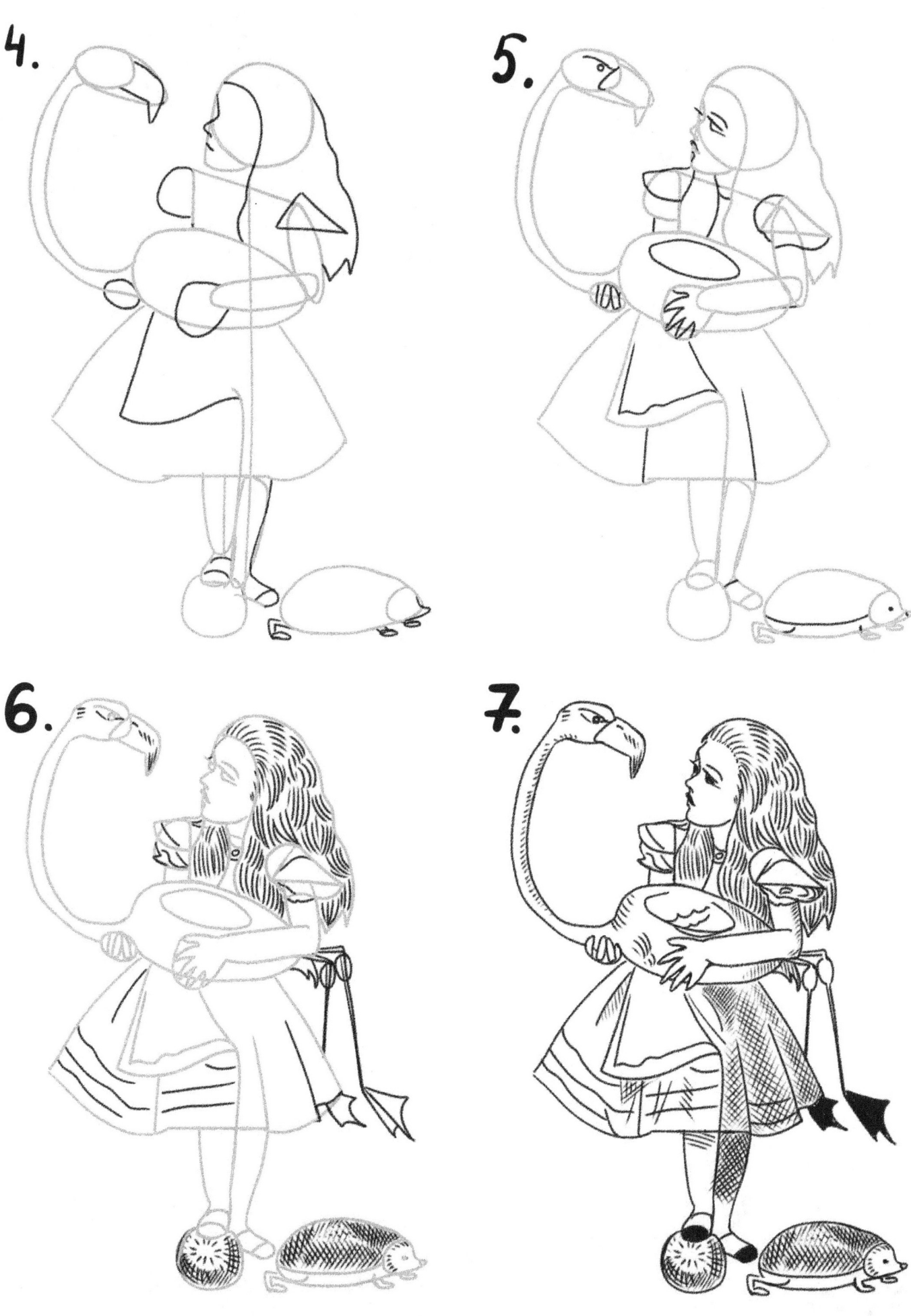

4.

5.

6.

7.